A Composition

Of

100 Radical Poems

and

100 Radical Haiku

By

Radical Rooney

The Century Collection

Radical Rooney

AuthorHouse™
1663 Liberty Drive, Suite 200
Bloomington, IN 47403
www.authorhouse.com
Phone: 1-800-839-8640

© 2009 Radical Rooney. All rights reserved.

No part of this book may be reproduced, stored in a retrieval system, or transmitted by any means without the written permission of the author.

First published by AuthorHouse 9/30/2009

ISBN: 978-1-4343-9172-8 (sc)
ISBN: 978-1-4343-9173-5 (hc)

Library of Congress Control Number: 2008904847

Printed in the United States of America
Bloomington, Indiana

This book is printed on acid-free paper.

For the hungry and the homeless.

The poet earns the nickname "Radical" by refusing to compromise in his rhetoric, while observing suffering through the eyes of a multitude of victims and persecutors.

Nearly all these poems are based on broad categories; life, love, tragedy, poverty, praise and so on. The poet prefers to write about specific actual events, including Hiroshima's destruction by the "Enola Gay" and the Kings Cross Tube tragedy, which is commemorated in a poem Prince Charles is said to have liked. The poet doesn't shy away from indicting a host of villains (by name) with his pen, or commemorating good people who met early demises. The structures feature end-rhymes and no punctual termination. The explanatory notes that accompany so many of the poems provide grounding content for each, notably improving comprehension and enjoyment.

Some of the least affected pieces are less about mass tragedies or widespread societal problems than they are about the despair of individuals. No one has ever erected a stature to those unfortunate enough to have survived failed eye surgery, but Radical Rooney puts the reader squarely inside the head of someone in that situation in "Dark for Me";

"When at noon the sun lit my life with fear, it was still dark,

And all that I could see, were dark explosions of mystery"

Walt Whitman's ebullient feeling of nostalgia in "Once I passed through a Populous City" is turned inside out in "The Runaway":

"As he stalked along the street, I saw his frightened face

When he entered slow this city, devoid of love or pity"

Though some poems ring of wonder or urge faith in God, outrage is most prevalent, and Rooney's outrage has an unfortunate tendency to steamroll the artistic balance. Some members of the IRA, animal testers at cosmetic companies, war loving Generals and others the poet opposes aren't outlined in complex portraits of positive qualities vying with flaws. Instead their unadulterated villainy is reinforced to the maximum, creating cartoonish figures who relish destruction.

His imaginative turns of phrase are arranged carefully enough, but he truly stands out for a limitless concern for all sorts of downtrodden classes and luckless bystanders. Rooney sees pain as unavoidable, writing "We must all suffer, for without pain there can't be, any compassion" as one of his Haiku. Cheers to this voice for the voiceless!   By Todd Mercer for Foreword Magazine.

Contents

Chapter 1 . . . . .Poems of Life 1

Chapter 2 . . . . .Poems of Love 13

Chapter 3 . . . . .Poems of Tragedy 25

Chapter 4 . . . . .Poems of Wonder 37

Chapter 5 . . . . .Poems of War 49

Chapter 6 . . . . .Poems of Animals 69

Chapter 7 . . . . .Poems of Poverty 81

Chapter 8 . . . . .Poems of Pain 95

Chapter 9 . . . . .Poems of Death 107

Chapter 10 . . . . .Poems of Praise 121

Chapter 11 . . . . .Huddle 1 135

Chapter 12 . . . . .Huddle 2 137

Chapter 13 . . . . .Huddle 3 139

Chapter 14 . . . . .Huddle 4 141

Chapter 15 . . . . .Huddle 5 143

Chapter 16 . . . . .Huddle 6 145

Chapter 17 . . . . .Huddle 7 147

Chapter 18 . . . . .Huddle 8 149

Chapter 19 . . . . .Huddle 9 151

Chapter 20 . . . . .Huddle 10 153

Tables of Poems

1. POEMS OF LIFE
Relics of the Past
Thru Factory Gates
The Train
With Water in My Eyes
The Norm
The Wrinkled Young
The Metaphysical Traveller
The Irony of Life
The Rasta - Ferry Man
Monkey Business

2. POEMS OF LOVE
Loves Return
For the Love of Dog
As One
Progeny
In Dreams
To Him Who Waits
Infatuation
Forgotten Love
First Born
Let Me Paint

3. POEMS OF TRAGEDY
The King's Cross Tube
Titanic
Culling of a Child
Ships in the Night
In the Cocktail Bar
Aberfan
The Hell of Heysel
The Disappeared
The Unsung Stranger
Nine - Eleven

4. POEMS OF WONDER
Autumn Leaves
The Final Harvest
The Key of the Door
I am Change, I am Life
Rainbows End
The Leaves in my Fire
I Fail to Understand
The Playground
Revelation
The Rose

5. POEMS OF WAR
Hiroshima
Auschwitz
The Truth of the Truce
Sad and Insane
The Wedding at Port Harcourt
Firestorm Over Dresden
Armageddon
Trilogy to the I.D.F.
Tides of Time
So Lucky

6. POEMS OF ANIMALS
Dominion of the Beast
A Canine Elegy
Tribute Á L'Oreal
I Am a Faroe - Islander
Slaughter of the Seals
Who Killed Mr Bee?
The Surrey Union Hunt
Where Wild Horses Graze
As of Hinges, As of Wheels
Epitaph to a Faithful Friend

7. POEMS OF POVERTY
Poverty
The Runaway
On His Own
Unemployed
The Immigrant
Her Usual Self
The Baby Smiles
Death of a Friend
The Phone-Box Boy
The World Passed By

8. POEMS OF PAIN
Letter to John
Loneliness
The Saga of Sarita
Ode to a Masochist
Failure
Animal Slights
Depression
Dark for Me
Courtroom Number Three
The Silence of the Sleeping Screws

9. POEMS OF DEATH
Dance of Death
Designer Death
The Accident
The Lift
For Them
My E-Type Jag
The Tree of Life
Tyburn Tree
The Watcher
Trilogy to a Foetus

10. POEMS OF PRAISE

God so Loved the World
I Don't Remember Singing
When the Saints go Marching In
The Age of Reason
I See You
Evil In - Evil Out
Show Me, Lord
For the Love of God
An Alien God
Bless This Day

Chapter 1
Poems of Life

RELICS OF THE PAST
THRU FACTORY GATES
THE TRAIN
WITH WATER IN MY EYES
THE NORM
THE WRINKLED YOUNG
THE METAPHYSICAL TRAVELLER
THE IRONY OF LIFE
THE RASTA - FERRY MAN
MONKEY BUSINESS

Relics of the Past

The last time I found peace
Was in the Children's Ward
Awake at night with my frozen foot
Back in the old country
Where the good old days
Saw steam trains journey slow
Into an age of Diesel
And it was there
Where I would lie awake at night
And listen hard to those fiery dragons
Perched impatiently, on distant tracks
Snorting mournful at the moon
Or sadly at some signal box
Reclining in another world
A coloured world, of light and glass
And I would hear these monsters gallop
Through the dark and rain, their metal hooves
Beating out my pain, as they whistled
Full of sorrow for their lovers
Lost and lonely in the night
But come the dawn and light
Their song was always lost to me
In the muffled call of pigeons
Cradling a new day, in gurgles of sympathy
For the old iron pipes that warmed the ward
And through the whitened stainéd glass
Of our little world, I too would raise
Mine eyes to the roof
And cry with envy, for their life
In a rooftop gutter, filled with snow
For I sensed that they were happy
With frozen feet, and little food
Whilst the trains and I, alas
Being relics of the past, were not

Thru Factory Gates

So much older, wiser too
Those hidden martyrs now are few
For lifeblood spilled, by tooth and claw
Did slowly drain, as thru a straw
And yet by stealth, I had to stay
My weekly wealth spent, day by day
To make me still a servile slave
As I too swung that creaking door
And stalked that same familiar floor
To the tuneless tick of time
Drawing fettered feet that did not shine
Thru factory gates, that still corrode
The souls that slave in her abode
But they now cage a different breed
Whose hopes of freedom fall as seed
To drift upon the wind of chance
All souls now sold without a glance
They find no offer of escape
As memory fades in routine rape
For other mouths must feed, and other shoes
Must fit, on other feet, to spread the news
That wheels with arms, unlike their own
Can always be replaced, or sown
As endless orders, drifting down
Do streams of sweat their bodies crown
While faceless strangers in some tower
Wield their wands of ruthless power -
Now twilight fades the workers hopes
As homeward bound down concrete slopes
They hear the songs of Gods afar
Come laughing thru those gates ajar

DEDICATED TO WESTINGHOUSE BRAKE AND SIGNAL CO.

The Train

Here I rest, a rusting hulk
Alone, aloof, within my bulk
The hiss of steam within my veins
The pistons pulling at the reins
Mere memories now of a loyal life
Now round my rivets rust is rife
No clank of coal, no whistle shout
No churning wheels, no water spout
Now rust flakes fast to line my grave
Where only leaves and litter pave
This epitaph to a faithful slave
And don't deny I served you well
Yet now condemned within my cell
Of rusted rails that bind me fast
Those guiding hands of days long past
When smells of grease and hissing steam
Echoed gleams and children's screams
As stones and steel rushed past my head
Now tears of rain make up this bed
A burial cloak for a servant laid
To rest and rust in romance dead

With Water in My Eyes

I moved to town, and the people came
And stole from me

They took the brightness from my life
And the colour from my skies
They stole the pity from my eyes
And the fur from off my cat
They killed my pride and crippled my beliefs
Then buried my love and planted seeds of lust

They used my body to poison my mind
And then they took my soul
And slowly crushed it dry
Now my skin grows thicker by the hour
My heart lies coated with envy
And I have learnt the power of hate

Now they own my body and my mind
Yet I feel so very strange
For my hungry hollow shell
That wanders home at night
Sometimes sees the stars
And I must lean against the wall

For I do not see so very well
With water in my eyes

The Norm

If you've got a hare-lip or a squint in your eye
Every day of your life you may just wish to die
For your brothers and sisters will offer you scorn
And you may even wish that you'd never been born
If you're a bit of a rebel and don't do what you're told
You'll need to be brave and you'll need to be bold
Or you'll be cast aside by the young and the old
And soon find yourself left out in the cold
But if you really do want to be part of the game
Make sure when you're born that you look just the same
As your brothers and sisters, so they'll call you by name

The Wrinkled Young

Youth is wasted on the young
They should be born with bodies hung
Of heaving lung, and stiff arthritis
And wrinkled ears, that sport tinnitus
But as they grow up, day by day
They should mature in every way
Learning wisdom and compassion
As they reap life's painful ration
To suffer fools then, they would learn
That others they must never spurn
And as they grow up day by day
They'd get wiser as they play
Their bodies would recover vigour
As they learnt to handle rigour
Infirmities would fade, hearing would improve
As vision sharpened up, their wrinkles now would smooth
Their hair would lose its grey and age would have its day
We'd see a world of wisdom, where lasting strength would pave
A just and patient world, from birth unto the grave

The Metaphysical Traveller

As my emotions hide in dreams
Masked enigmas probe the seams
Winding round like tears of death
Losing hope with fading breath
But their potent piercing passes
As fatalistic evil masses
Weave their timeless images
In tilting towers of thought
And as my longing lingers
Some sad serene and weary dream
Left uncloaked in hollow smoke
Paints portraits of my soul
On barren rocks so cold
The oracle doth call
To mask those waiting dreams
It shrieks and screams to fall
In sloping groping shadows
Where the prodigal voice of hate
Beckons home like fate
Those riding by to feed
The frozen statue that is greed
Then turns my way, to slowly bleed

The Irony of Life

How in life may one man spy
Where drifting dust on each may lie
Fickle fate alone may tell
Where by design that dust may dwell
Fast casting spells like flaking lead
Unfailing favour for each head
So timeless pains must fall on each
Soft shadowed soul within its reach
As grinding on this wheel of fate
Spins tears of joy to tears of hate
And yet unheeding to its call
We end up victims as we fall
And stumble into ashes deep
To kindle them in hope of sleep
Yet some remain who standing still
Find wonder in the will of Him
Who sprinkles dust with careless whim

The Rasta-ferry Man

I'm a Rasta man, I ain't no thug
I smoke a little weed, but it ain't no drug
Don't want no hassle, don't want no aid
Ain't got no job, so me don't get paid
But a like a little sound and a like a little smoke
A like a little girl and a like a little joke
I'll drink when I'm dry and I'll eat when I need
A don't need no grief, a don't need no speed
Am stuck in this place which is all wet and cold
A can't escape England, for me soul she is sold

Monkey Business

She was a real artist in true classic form
Spending many a day making colours conform
Painting sunsets and seas that took many hours
And even old trees, or vases of flowers

With news these fine efforts would simply not pay
She accepted the muse of the modern art way
Having loved all Picassos she dillied with Dali
But found those in the know around her would rally

Stating simply she wandered alone in a void
They stayed vexed and perplexed and even annoyed
In her stance, that pure art should be simply perceived
But these vultures of culture would not be deceived

They rejected all sense of her talent and skill
And claimed a true artist must destiny fill
A blank canvas, with splodges of dabbles and dots
And splurges of colour, that gave them the hots

Not arcane or archaic but simply obtuse
So lickspittle morons could have no excuse
Than to drool and to fawn as they all got their kicks
Seeing dirty old knicks on dirty old bricks

Your quintessential essence must not cloud the air
So swallow up your ego, she heard them all declare
For status and for power, display a blinding effluence
So we can see your taste, decay away with affluence

I mean, Congo the Chimp sells for over ten grand
He may be a monkey, but he's gathered a band
Of faithful old fauvists, all trying to look smart
As they burp and they fart to this primal art

So these prophets of doom made her paint on in hell
Now their own troubled minds could suffer as well
Like old dogs in heat they would ogle and claw
To view any old spawn from this prostitutes paw

Standing drinking, round her painting, in reflected glory
Gleaning meaning, so bizarre, it verged upon the gory
But kindergarten sprawls offered psueds a-sunder
All a chance to sense pretense, and float in naive wonder

Upon this vulgar altar where she offered up contention
As anointed cognoscenti waved away convention
So her new renaissance could make it's presentation
Making monied monkey-art, in utter ostentation

DEDICATED TO MY DEAR FRIEND
SONIA VENESS. BA. MA. ARTS

Chapter 2
Poems of Love

LOVES RETURN
FOR THE LOVE OF DOG
AS ONE
PROGENY
IN DREAMS
TO HIM WHO WAITS
INFATUATION
FORGOTTEN LOVE
FIRST BORN
LET ME PAINT

Loves Return

Where goes my love, for as she wanders
Minutes, seconds, hours she squanders
Yet this goddess carved in flesh
Must soon be caught within my mesh
As echoed footsteps, brisk and fast
Cast mottled shadows on the glass
Flitting figures of mere mortals
Fleeting shadows on my portals
Would that she could grace my door
As to her touch my soul would soar
To mould again this beauty fair
To sense the sacred vision there
Yet now my heart grows cold with fear
Without her healing presence here
This hunger she has carved so deep
Dares not grant my spirit sleep
For this fire that slowly burns
Must consume lest she returns

For the Love of Dog

How noble is this humble dog
As he sleeps here, like the log
Beside the fire, beside the grate
Devoid of guilt, devoid of hate
He earns respect and not neglect
But as he sleeps at my feet, curled
I sense the anger of a world
Where wretches there
Who'd hurt and harm
A single hair upon his head
Need lead a life of prayer and charm
Else they should wish that they be dead
For I'd not rest, put to the test
But now, he hovers in his sleep
Perfection, in his breathing deep
His little chest seems so at rest
But could it be, he may not wake
Why then, my very soul would quake
And I should drown in misery
So surely now, asleep he be
And yet I know that day will come
So slowly, like the setting sun
But now he stirs, to lick my face
And condescends to join the race
As to my talk of winter walk
Decides to join the merry throng
As bounding round he sings his song
But in this life I never knew
That trust and love could be so true
Such lust of life that must consume
Like innocence within the womb

As One

Could you cast your net above me
Would you let its power enfold me
To let it bring me, oh so gently
All the charms sweet nature lent thee
Would we in soul and spirit too
Then as one, share love so true
Where single loves we lived as two
As one my love would live in you

Progeny

This day in your life you created another
From this day on, they will know you as mother
In years to come there will always be one
To tell the world that you bore a son
He'll tell them all that you gave him birth
By him will they know, you too lived on earth
And when you have gone you'll leave something behind
For you still will live on, in somebody's mind
They will survive you, all won't be in vain
They'll be there at your grave, in sunshine or rain

In Dreams

That silken gaze within your eyes
Doth lure me deep, in soft surprise
As silken lips give voice so tender
Silence cries for loves surrender
To sink into your golden tresses
And whisper slowly soft caresses
To this song of lullabies
My spirit soars in loving sighs
Let hearts enfold and souls entwine
In precious dreams I'll make you mine

To Him Who Waits

Shadows of the past, while whispering recall
The way he always sought escape, from people one and all
But the silence of his stillness stirs the freshness in her tears
As she wanders, waiting wonders, sounds of saviours, no one hears
So solace seeking, softly searching, she wanders by the mill
To hear its song of sadness, while it slowly turned
Calling her to join him, where love is never spurned
So to the spinning of the wheel, she whispers as it turns
If only she could see and feel, this love for which she yearns
She struggles not, she feels no fear, she knows her fate is cast
When his voice, so clear and calm, cries out she's his at last

Infatuation

Infatuation, when it ripens, unrequited love
Is like the lily, in the valley, washed away with rain
But blossoms fair fall again, in those hills above
As sweet flowers wane, to grow again, as this dream of love
Ripens roots, buried deep, where buds of life still grow
In gentle sleep, but pain will wane, for carried from above
Streams of hope will surely grow, from this dream of love

Forgotten Love

Some loving voice within me cries
As to my soul a song it sighs
My thoughts revolve around romancing
In my mind a maiden fair
The rustic leaves of autumn dancing
Weave the beauty in her hair

This mystic love can touch the skies
For aloft on wings it flies
As my spirit soars like silken dove
Bearing thoughts of sacred love
But now I grieve, for in my mind
Dark sorrow chokes me, love is blind

Yet in death is there life
And in blindness a light
As my soul bears a love that burning bright
Sheds tears of joy to the stars of night
Some children laugh as an old man cries
A baby sleeps as a young boy dies

But my spirit warms with memories dear
As I find again her presence is near
For I sense that day when love has gone
In the mists of time that linger on
Our very souls will search out love
When our candles burn in the skies above

First Born

Not in the wildest dreams above
Could I dream such mystic love
As this love I shed for you
A love of pride, and pity too
For not until you were created
Could I feel at all elated
No, not 'til you were given birth
Could I love you on this earth

Let Me Paint

A sky with your smile
A world with your wonder
My heart with your hope
And my life with your love

Chapter 3
Poems of Tragedy

THE KING'S CROSS TUBE
TITANIC
CULLING OF A CHILD
SHIPS IN THE NIGHT
IN THE COCKTAIL BAR
ABERFAN
THE HELL OF HEYSEL
THE DISAPPEARED
THE UNSUNG STRANGER
NINE – ELEVEN

The Kings Cross Tube

IN DECEMBER 1987 THIS POEM WAS INSCRIBED ONTO PARCHMENT AND MOUNTED BEHIND A LARGE GLASS SCREEN TO BE DISPLAYED FOR MANY MONTHS, WITH THE COUNTLESS OTHER TRIBUTES OUTSIDE KINGS CROSS STATION. IT WAS LATER READ ON SOUTHERN SOUND RADIO, AND ON SEEING THE POEM, H.R.H. PRINCE CHARLES COMMENTED FAVOURABLY.

For the people, starting another day
The Kings Cross Tube clanked on its way
Six hundred souls crushed together
A silent six hundred rushed together
As doors clamped shut, their eyes grew slack
They gazed at the lights but the bulbs stared back

They crinkled their papers and buried their heads
And smelt the stale air and thought of their beds
But then the six hundred slowed to a stop
For deep in the earth at an unknown spot
The Kings Cross Tube ground to a halt
Not a word was heard as they all held their breath
Were the silent six hundred waiting for death

Like leeches they clung, as one by one
On metal springs their bodies hung
They raised their heads but the silence bit deep
It clawed at their souls as they shuffled their feet
Then the brakes gave a sigh and the motors hummed
The Kings Cross Tube clanked on its way
For the people starting another day

It thundered on to arrive at the station
Where they all rushed out of this metal creation
To push up the platform and squeeze round the bend
Where they stood on a staircase without any end
Habit had trained them to stand on the right
So each stood on a step and gazed at the sight
Of billowing smoke from the staircase well
That ushered them into a living hell
Where they fought for life beneath the street
A battle blind, in the fumes and the heat
That stole them away, their Maker to meet

DEDICATED TO THE 31 VICTIMS

Titanic

This sad story I was told
By an ancient shipwright, old and bold
Who built a boat, in Belfast town
That saw some thousand people drown
We showed our skill, we had such pride
As we gazed upon her cliff-like side
By painting on the hull below
Where strangers eyes would never go
Immortal words that touched the lip
"Even God can't sink this ship"
For in our skill we put such trust
Not knowing that the Earth's crust
As it formed the ore, the ship to mould
Gathered snowflakes in the cold
To form the iceberg, that in time
Would be drawn, as thou by line
To dark caress, as cold and still
These lovers echoed cries so shrill
That their caress, in dead of night
Did break their backs, despite their might
But when in pride, we wrote such things
We found that God, all sorrow brings
So be warned when wielding skill
You do submit to Gods own will

The Culling of a Child

IN RIO-DE-JANEIRO A MILLION CHILDREN LIVE ROUGH ON THE STREETS. THEY SURVIVE BY BEGGING AND STEALING AND THIS HAS PROMPTED THE RICH SHOP-OWNERS TO EMPLOY DEATH SQUADS, TO PROTECT THEIR LAVISH LIFE-STYLE, WHO SLAUGHTER HUNDREDS OF CHILDREN A MONTH, BY POURING PETROL DOWN THE SEWERS, WHERE THEY SLEEP, OR GUNNING THEM DOWN WHERE THEY FIND THEM BY DAY, LIVING ON WASTELAND.

Do not fear, and do not weep
For us, the children of the street
Who flourish in this no-mans land
Where poverty and riches meet
We are one people, you and me
Your future lives in us
But as you kill you cannot see
The beauty you destroy
For when you slaughter children
With natures wrath you toy
For as innocents are culled
And pavements warm their breath
The tourists then are lulled
To sponsor sudden death
In sewers and alleys, look around
We live and die on wasted ground
For killers placed in tinsel town
By the devils of desire
Send Godless slaves to shoot us down
In a blaze of rich mans fire

Ships in the Night

ON SUNDAY 27TH MARCH 1977 TWO JUMBO JETS COLLIDED, IN BLINDING SNOW AT TENERIFE AIRPORT. SIX HUNDRED PERISHED IN THE WORST AIR DISASTER EVER RECORDED

Suzie and the captain cried
When they heard six hundred died
In silver ships that did not pass
As in the night they met, alas

With no-one left to shoulder guilt
This sorrow will not ever wilt
All blame was hidden in the snow
Whose fault it was, no one will know

But even though the pain is past
Reality and death outlast
Those secrets buried 'neath the snow
Where love has died and guilt will grow

TO SUZIE, A BRITISH CALEDONIAN STEWARDESS

In the Cocktail Bar

They looked, with dark glasses and shades
As the boss said, a couple of right tasty blades
Pete, the Para and Lee, of the old R.U.C
Were getting blind drunk, quite literally
For being blown up, in Ireland, left a sad memory
And Pete who taught Judo now, said 'never mind'
The only ones I can't teach, these days, are the blind
So we all laughed out loud, 'til Lee turned and said
Now I can't watch T.V., I just listen instead
But I remember the time we were blown to the floor
And the bloke down the road heard this thump on his door
So he ran round and found, in the rain and the sleet
The head of my mate, lying right at his feet
Well, I think we were lucky, said Pete, butting in
That we didn't end up dead meat, in the bin
So they clung to the bar, swaying around in the heat
Their faithful old guide dogs asleep at their feet

WITH APOLOGIES AND AFFECTION TO LEE AND MARTIN OF ST.DUNSTANS HOME FOR THE BLIND, SUSSEX, ENGLAND.

Aberfan

IN 1989 THE NATIONAL COAL BOARD CLOSED THE COAL-PIT AT ABERFAN. THE VILLAGE SLOWLY DIED AND WITH IT THE MEMORY OF A WHOLE GENERATION OF CHILDREN WHO PERISHED, WHEN THE GIGANTIC SLAGHEAP OF THE COAL-TIP SLID DOWN IN HEAVY RAIN UPON THE VILLAGE SCHOOL. THE ONE HUNDRED AND SIXTEEN CHILDREN WERE ALL AGED BETWEEN EIGHT AND TEN YEARS OLD.

By the black heaps of slag
Were they born
From the coal-tip black
Were they carved
Out the desecrated land
Were they reared
Side the smouldering slime
Were they shamed
And 'neath the landscape raped
Were they buried

The Hell of Heysel

IN 1985 IN THE HEYSEL STADIUM, IN ITALY, ON THE 29ᵀᴴ MAY, THIRTY-NINE PEOPLE PERISHED AT THE HANDS OF MINDLESS FOOTBALL FANATICS WHEN A CONTINGENT OF LIVERPOOL FANS DELIBERATELY STAMPEDED TOWARDS THE OPPOSING SUPPORTERS. EVEN THE SCALE OF THE DISASTER DID NOT MEAN THE MATCH WOULD BE POSTPONED; AUTHORITIES DECIDED AGAINST THIS BECAUSE THEY FEARED EVEN MORE DISRUPTION IF THE EVENT WAS CANCELLED.

'Ere we go, 'ere we go, 'ere we go
We tell 'em all where to go, where to go

Pubs all shut, and traffic stops
Strength of numbers halts the cops

We're off to kill and crush and maim
It's what we call the football game

We shove and spit and bottle folks
We're full of fun, full of jokes

We got no tickets, never mind
With push and shove we all find
The gates'll open, ain't they kind

But kiddies, children, women too
End up screaming, turning blue
Against the fence, with no way through

But as we push on with our mates
We spot some blokes resuscitate
So we stand back and urinate

But they carry on, to play the game
With punters down there, dying in shame

So we laugh, and live up to our name
To us, it's just a football game

The Disappeared

No eyes were dry in the street that day
When a lone sniper shot for the I.R.A.
A teenage soldier who cried for his mum
As he bled to his death, in the morning sun
Jean McConville gently cradled his head
As he called for his mum until he lay dead
Jean knew what it was to be so alone
She'd brought up ten children all on her own
Catholic women should just lure soldiers to death
Not give them comfort, in their dying breath
Gerry Adams gave orders, Jean must disappear
So the Turf-Lodge Gang shot her right in the ear
Then stuck her in sand, down by the water
If no-one could find her, he could deny slaughter
But Bill said to Gerry, "you've got bad exposure
Ten orphans want a body back, so they can have closure
So dig her up, send her back, then you won't get such flack"
"But the kids are all in foster homes," Gerry said at last
"And if we leave her in the sand, the tide will rot her fast
But I don't really care, nor need a reason why
For my Kangaroo Court had sentenced her to die
Now I know she wasn't there, and didn't stand a prayer
But when this scandal goes away, we can kill another day."

DEDICATED TO THE THREE YOUNG CATHOLIC WOMEN WHO LURED THREE SOLDIERS TO THEIR DEATH, AND OF COURSE, GERRY ADAMS AND BILL CLINTON.

The Unsung Stranger

DEDICATED TO THE UNSUNG STRANGER, FOUND IN THE BOOKING HALL, AFTER THE KINGS CROSS UNDERGROUND DISASTER WHO, EVEN WITH A SURGICAL PLATE IN HIS SKULL AND STENCILLED TEETH, TO THIS DAY STILL DEFIES IDENTIFICATION.

No marker for my grave
No wreaths, no relatives
Only my old friend, pain
But I too was there, I too burned
I too, watched the great ball of fire
As it spawned and swirled
Around this evil hall of death
I too, saw it bounce off wall and ceiling
As it roared around the room
Eating up the innocent
I too, smelt the stench of burning flesh
I too, held out melting hands for its embrace
I too, heard the prayers and screams, all cease
And I too, died that night, in Hell
But my ghost, my un-named ghost
Lies waiting for the guilty to unite
And taste the taste of Hell
As they dwell with us this night

Nine Eleven

I was stunned as I gazed at the clear blue sky
For I sat there amazed, just wondering why
A plane did appear to suddenly fly
Straight toward me, as I stared out on high
I watched it glide in so low and so fast
And fear gripped my soul to see it fly past
To pierce like an arrow the opposite tower
And explode in a blast of gigantic power
Immersing itself in a molten maze
And covering all with a massive blaze
But as we watched on in sheer disbelief
We sank into shame, inside all our grief
Watching those human fireballs fall
Hearing no scream, hearing no call
'Til a second plane flew into sight
And our shock and our shame reverted to fright
As death cloaked us all on that fateful day
In a strange, surreal and selfish way
We stood and we watched as the other tower collapsed
And any hope we had left then suddenly lapsed
As we all seemed to sense we were now on our own
And rushed round in panic, to find a free phone
To utter our love, to our friends one and all
We surrendered our souls, in that last final call
As we spoke of the things that we just could not say
In the cold and the callous light of the day
We pledged all our love, and then said goodbye
We fell to our knees, and we waited to die
But even then, as our world fell apart
We turned to our God, with love in our heart

DEDICATED TO THE THREE THOUSAND

Chapter 4
Poems of Wonder

AUTUMN LEAVES
THE FINAL HARVEST
THE KEY OF THE DOOR
I AM CHANGE, I AM LIFE
RAINBOWS END
THE LEAVES IN MY FIRE
I FAIL TO UNDERSTAND
THE PLAYGROUND
REVELATION
THE ROSE

Autumn Leaves

As drops of dew to leaves are lent
They sparkle in the autumn scent
As round these trees like voices calling
Leaves blow slow in silence falling

The Final Harvest

When you just cannot see, for the tears in your eyes
And all of your friends ignore all your cries
When you feel that of troubles the burden you bear
Weighs more than it should, much more than your share
Look round you and think, if we all had romance
If we all had equal share and all had equal chance
Our ultimate rewards would all be equal too
And there'd be no point of life for me or for you
Therefore our reward depends, on what luck we get
The way that we use it, and the way that we let
Our little lives slip by, so please do not forget
That if you don't reap rewards on this earth, my friend
You'll be well compensated in the harvest at the end

The Key of the Door

There are many keys to the doorway of fame
Not carved or engraved with any one name
But we all have a few in the gifts we possess
And one of those keys should give us success
But to find the right key is the secret of life
To find peace amidst worry and flurry and strife
For though we grow old and time stands to mock
We may still have the key that will open the lock
For the very thing that may open that door
May be the key that we've tried out before

I Am Change, I Am Life

I am all things, to all men

I am the spring of youth
Hope awaiting help
And the singer in the song

I am the leper leaving life
A cancer cutting clean
And a writer carving thought

I am the draw of the crowd
The madness in the soul
And the child that knows no name

I am a maiden after beauty
A harlot into innocence
And a virgin waiting lovers

I am music teasing silence
Where lovers test their oneness
And a drunk without power

I am the redness in the blood
Of a lady looking lovely
And a woman wearing weals

I am the pressure in the weight
The aching in the brain
And the shadow in the light

I am the good within
And the evil without
Every saint and every sinner

I am every hammock hanging
Every hangman grieving
And everyman, alone

I am all things, to all men
I am change, I am life

Rainbows End

Where falls this misty rain to show
Long ribboned rays where rainbows glow
Through silken clouds where shadows flow
In golden beams they slowly grow

To light my life with colours free
Leaving signs of peace for me
This memory of Gods love will be
A golden message all should see

The Leaves in My Fire

That cried as they died in the wind, made the mask of my mind unwind
    To fall afresh from off my face, as like the fire my senses roared
    So the smoke in spirals soared, in dark defences drifting down
Around the winding winds it wound, the shafts of sunlight that it found
    To pierce and penetrate in parts, this rhythm as a rainbow raw
    Which waxed and waned within, the sudden shadows that it shifted
    In and out the shapes it sifted, and as I watched and wondered

    In skies above I did perceive, a plane did on the ether freeze
    Itself a sudden space in time, to slice inside the thinning skies
    A shinning silver soft surprise, but sliding silent those up there
Could only guess at all the splendour, they were soaked in thoughts elsewhere
    Just then I spied a frightened face, attracted by my fire, I feared
    A fox that felt, just like me forced, into this hungry city, sensed
    To keep on scratching all the more, just meant the greater grew the sore

I Fail to Understand

I fail to understand, oh Lord
Why your world has grown in many places
So blasé and complicated
Like the science of shoes or the enigma of laces
Which seem to get so intricated

I fail to understand, oh Lord
The arrogance that makes men think
They never will destroy this world
Even when it's on the brink
As all the cars and chimneys spout
And all the ozone oozes out
As ice caps start to melt
And rising heat is felt

I fail to understand, oh Lord
Why in the skies above
I simply cannot love
Or even for a moment, be
The creature that is simply, me

The Playground

Drifting near this winters eve
I faintly hear some children weave
A serenade, a song they sing
That floats upon the wind to bring
A lilting tune that drifts and falls
As gliding round it faintly calls
The fading echo of a name
As memory plays a children's game

Revelation

Each one of us is born
Quite without care
So beautiful, so perfect
So sinfully aware
But as we grow
The blossom fades
And as we go
We sense the shades
Of distant memory
In the caves
Of religion and belief
But in the murky mists of time
As loving memories we recall
Within the past there lives a sign
Of self awareness as we fall
To where the God within us all
Lies dormant, waiting for our call

The Rose

Her heart with fragrant beauty shows
The womb her silken hands enclose
But curling fingers edged with gold
Must wither soon as they grow old
And as her petals curl with age
To gently fall like turning page
They will in memory oft' repeat
To us a scent that lingers sweet

Chapter 5
Poems of War

HIROSHIMA
AUSCHWITZ
THE TRUTH OF THE TRUCE
SAD AND INSANE
THE WEDDING AT PORT HARCOURT
FIRESTORM OVER DRESDEN
ARMAGEDDON
TRILOGY OF THE I.D.F.
TIDES OF TIME
SO LUCKY

Hiroshima

I remember it well, that first day in Hell
So long ago, I know

As the sirens sounded our Yankee foe
Decided that now, his power we would know
So dropped his Atomic Bomb from the sky
That caused those below to melt and to fry
We all saw the flash and then felt the blast
That blew infernos around us, to eerily cast
A different light on a different world
As blackened bodies lay unfurled
In corners and gutters clinging together
Welded and wedded where no man could sever

Yet skinless souls still shuffled by
In silent circles they would try
To see the sun, to see the sky

I remember it well, that first day in Hell
So long ago, I know

When God let man his fate create
And Genius fell to earth, as hate
As dependant on a Compass whim
Determined how much blackened skin
Would flap around, about your heel
Or even how much pain you'd feel
As you dragged around your cloak of death
Blinded, deafened, sucking breath
Those with huge bloated heads just staggered around
'Til their eyeballs popped out, to explode on the ground

The Mushroom cloud now rose on high
As snow-like ashes fell to lie
On those below who searched the sky

I remember it well, that first day in Hell
So long ago, I know

I watched where tender lips did lie
To see dark holes vent silent cry
I saw the shape of a horse, as he stood in the Sun
To bask in God's warmth, 'til a hotter one
Burnt him so perfect, against a white wall
In an instant heat, that left no time to fall
I saw shadows on steps, where bodies had curled
As vaporized souls left their mark on this world
Now black dollops of rain fell out of the mist
From that curse`d sky in one final twist

But the deaf and the blind who looked up to God
Found these cascades of rain were naught but a fraud
For they fell with the splash of hot nuclear ash

I remember it well, that first day in Hell
So long ago, I know

Then we dug in the rubble, the debris to hurl
And managed to find a frail little girl
It dampened our glee, when she just couldn't see
But still managed to cry, thru one squid-like eye
Whose last look at life was facing the Sun
That once gave her birth, but then fell to Earth
So feeling her pain on that lonely day
I stroked her long hair, 'til I felt her sway
As it fell out in clumps, and looked really bad
For although she was blind, she felt really sad

Then our saviours arrived with water and food
But no victims of burns should drink, if they could
So they gasped and gave up, and dropped where they stood

I remember it well, that first day in Hell
So long ago, I know

This child that we found needed blood, so my friend
Decided to give, being so close to the end
So he gave what he could though feeling so feeble
But couldn't stop bleeding when they took out the needle
He had just drunk too much of that evil black rain
So we stood by in shame, as he gave up his pain.
In the centre of town stood a fountain and pond
Thirsty circles clung there, 'til Death waved her wand
Now they sit in my mind, but at night circle round
Like those in the fires, who dug into the ground

The firestorm had started to eat up the air
Yet many stood still, for they just didn't care
But most panicked in fear, and ran here and ran there

I remember it well, that first day in Hell
So long ago, I know

So we ran to the river but the river ran red
As thousands jumped in, as they burned and they bled
But they drowned in the scrum, and ended up dead
As corpses and bodies to the surface were fed
Our nails and our teeth and our hair then fell out
While those trapped in the fires screamed shout after shout
The day that huge plane dropped a gift with regret
A gift to remember, a gift to forget
When it placed Hell on Earth, and our City ceased
With a toast from the skies, and a boast from the beast

DEDICATED TO LITTLE TAEKAKO YOSHIMOTO, ONE OF THREE THOUSAND SCHOOLCHILDREN WHO PERISHED THAT FIRST DAY IN HELL

Auschwitz

As I shuffle, as I shift
The tons of ashes slowly drift
As tens of thousands daily dead
To the pit are quickly fed
In flaming fires where pain is passed
And love alone survives the fast
As barbed wire beckons sleep
So shaven ladies leap
To where electric fences reap
Burnt rewards for fleet of feet
Now freed from tolling life's grim bell
Now freed from out this living hell
To where their souls delivered free
Can seek some bleak eternity
They wander in a blackened cave
They wallow in an empty grave
They sadly sink in freedoms womb
To gladly walk into the tomb
Where furnace chimneys smoke above
And clouds of life drift off like love

**DEDICATED TO THE ONE MILLION JEWS
WHO PERISHED IN THIS CAMP ALONE.**

The Truth of the Truce

Buried in stench, deep down in our trench
We dream of our bed and wish we were dead
For we hear all the wails as we chew on our nails
And munch our plum puddings as hard as a brick
While we fight in this war, feeling so sick
For the innocent men who must die every day
So General Haig can have his own way
But we're not the ones, to even ask why
Just run for the Hun, and hope not to die
But suddenly Christmas comes marching along
And some of the Germans burst into song
A candlelit tree near our front line they carried
As they sang Silent Night, around us they scurried
But they staggered along, for they just couldn't see
Thru the flurries of snow where the trenches should be
But then Private Richards dug deep in the mud
And flung them a pudding all covered in blood
But when they returned with cases of beer
We lost all our anger and drowned out our fear
The officers all then agreed a reprieve
So the men could rejoice on this cold Christmas Eve
Then we laid down our dead, in bleak no-mans land
To the mournful tune of a lone Piper Band
As gifts were exchanged simple logic explained
Why this truce should not end with the gifts we did send
But General Haig then panicked in fright
When he found half his Army just wouldn't fight
So out in the snow in the dead of the night
To slaughter some soldier, a sniper he sent
Who soon found a target, for the truce now was rent
As big guns erupted and peace slowly passed
The top brass corrupted to make the war last

But what did they gain, no one will know
As hordes of our heroes dropped down like the snow
Why this carnage continued just isn't clear
For they slaughtered a million, year after year
But we who survived will never forget
That fateful day when two armies met
We all will remember that cold Christmas Eve
When late one December, in God we believed.

DEDICATED TO PRIVATE FRANK RICHARDS

Sad and Insane

I'm not sad or insane
I'm just Saddam Hussein
But I hate all those Kurds
Who float round like turds
For they live in a marsh
And although it sounds harsh
I will dose 'em with gas
'Til their nerves all wither
Then laugh as they drop
To slurp and to slither
I'll choke off their lungs
And poison their blood
And then grind their children
All into the mud
I will bomb them and napalm them
Then bury and embalm them
For to me it seems right
To slaughter them all
By day, or by night

DEDICATED TO SADDAM'S COUSIN ALI HASSAN AL-MAJID, ALSO KNOWN AS CHEMICAL ALI, RESPONSIBLE FOR THE CHEMICAL GASSING OF FIVE THOUSAND MEN, WOMEN AND CHILDREN IN THE KURDISH CITY OF HALABJAH

The Wedding at Port Harcourt

DURING THE CIVIL WAR IN NIGERIA, COMMANDER ALBERT DIETE SPIFF CELEBRATED HIS WEDDING IN PORT HARCOURT ONLY TWO MILES FROM WHERE THOUSANDS OF IBO CHILDREN WERE STARVING TO DEATH. A REPRESENTATIVE OF THE BRITISH GOVERNMENT, LORD HUNT, SENT THERE TO REVIEW THE FAMINE, CLAIMED THE SITUATION WAS 'NOT TOO BAD'. IT IS NOT KNOWN IF HE WAS ONE OF THE TWO HUNDRED DIGNITARIES AT THE WEDDING, BUT PERHAPS THE LAVISH EXPENSE OF THE PROCEEDINGS INFLUENCED HIM INTO THINKING THE CRISIS WAS NOT AS BAD AS THE PRESS CLAIMED.

It was
A lovely little wedding
Not white, black, but
With all the local dignitaries
But no Lords, and Albert
So wanted a Lord
I had to tell him
Not many left. Expensive

There were
Lots of Pigs and Goats
But not many Lords;
Especially British Lords
Albert burped and drank
Another Scotch; he should have
Stuck to Champagne, but
Those turkeys, barbecued

That is
Were excelled only by
The roasted piglets, and
The salads, oh those salads
That crisped and crunched
As we sat in circles sipping
We did not stop, not once, we
Could have, but we did not, once

Then we
All decided to go, wanted
To see, but Albert said that
Two miles is two, too far
Besides, if we stopped
And listened, we could hear
Them starve; not that
They made much noise

But on
The wind, we heard
Above the humming flies
The funny cries, the sighs
They carried well like
Smells of food, Albert said
We did not stop, not once, we
Could have, but we did not, once

Firestorm Over Dresden

In old Dresden City, where the girls were so pretty
We were running in fear because we could hear
Many planes in the night, and the terrible sight
Of thousands of bombs, as they sang out their songs
To fall just like rain, as we screamed out in pain
When tons of pure phosphor dropped down like snow
On the people below with nowhere to go
For they circled us all in a huge ring of fire
Which started to spiral, as it grew even higher
Our lungs just drained dry, as the fire soared on high
People burst into flames, but soon joined the dead
For into the firestorm their bodies were fed
As children and babies were just sucked away
When Hell fell on Earth, turning night into day
Pregnant women in shock, gave birth in the street
Induced by the noise, and the terrible heat
Horses were charcoaled, as they stood on their feet
So we jumped in canals, and started to pray
But the water boiled up, and baked us like clay
Bomber Harris had claimed his magnificent plan
Would destroy this fine city, down to a man
But some did survive to relate this great tale
Of the day human nature just seemed to fail
And total destruction was then made the aim
When wholescale war was the name of the game

DEDICATED TO THE 35,000 WHO DIED ON 13th FEBRUARY 1945 BY THE HAND OF BUTCHER HARRIS OF BOMBER COMMAND

Armageddon

A still wind rustles fate
As mushrooms naked blaze
Where skies of smoke create
Tall spirals in the haze
Now distant fireballs spawn
On cold and callous shores
And raging suns have split the dawn
In nuclear heat that bores
Into red flesh with deadly rays
To conjure silent screams
And man that toys with life these days
Must now live life in dreams

Trilogy to the I.D.F. (Israeli Defence Force) Part One

IN 2004 A SUICIDE BOMBER SLAUGHTERED TWO INNOCENT CHILDREN IN JERUSALEM. ISRAEL SWORE RETRIBUTION, AND BEGAN TO TARGET CHILDREN IN THE OCCUPIED TERRITORIES, FORGETTING THAT ONE ATROCITY DOES NOT EXCUSE ANOTHER. DEDICATED TO THE PLATOON COMMANDER OF THE GIVATI BRIGADE, WHO EMPTIED HIS MACHINE-GUN INTO THIRTEEN-YEAR-OLD IYMAN AL- HAMS, AS SHE LAY DYING IN THE STREET AND TO THE YOUNG ISRAELI SNIPER WHO SHOT AND KILLED ELEVEN-YEAR-OLD GHADIR MOKHEIMER AS SHE INNOCENTLY SAT AT HER SCHOOL-DESK IN A REFUGEE CAMP IN GAZA CITY.

> Feeling brave and feeling pretty
> As we carve up Gaza City
> We're heroes of the I.D.F.
> Killing kids and dishing death
> When we blow up a tenement block
> It's women and children who die in the shock
> And we don't feel bad when we gun down a kid
> For of suicide bombers we got to be rid
> But these practice targets are running out fast
> So we have to resort to shooting through glass
> Into classroom windows, where the kids learn to read
> But the rate that we kill 'em, there'll be few left to breed
> For we've polished off thirty, in a matter of days
> And just bagged a beauty on her way up to class
> As we shot her just once, when she came up to pass
> The heroes of the IDF
> Feeling brave and feeling pretty
> On their way through Gaza City
> Her rucksack, we felt, could have been a bomb
> But her shattered face sang a different song
> For when she got up she panicked in fear
> And ran straight for us; her heroes were near
> So we shot her again, as she screamed out in pain

Twenty bullets of lead, made sure she was dead
But in truth most of us shot her straight thru the head
Still, great target practice, this innocent death
For the butchers of the IDF
Feeling brave and feeling pretty
Like rats in a sewer, as we ravage the City.

**DEDICATED TO THE PLATOON COMMANDER
OF THE GIVATI BRIGADE
SPONSORED BY SAMUEL LEONARD MYERS. J.F.J.F.P
(*JEWS FOR JUSTICE FOR PALESTINIANS*)**

Trilogy to the I.D.F. (Israeli Defence Force) Part Two

IN MARCH 2003 A YOUNG AMERICAN PEACE ACTIVIST, RACHEL CORRIE, WENT TO THE GAZA STRIP TO HELP THE PALESTINIANS AS THE I.D.F. WERE DEMOLISHING 5000 HOMES IN THE PALESTINIAN TERRITORIES THEY WERE ILLEGALLY OCCUPYING. THE I.D.F. WERE USING AMERICAN SUPPLIED CATERPILLAR BULLDOZERS THAT WERE SPECIALLY ARMOURED BY THE AMERICAN COMPANY WHO SUPPLIED THEM; ALTHOUGH WITNESSES SWORE THE DRIVER OF THE GIANT MACHINE THAT CRUSHED RACHEL TO DEATH WAS VERY AWARE OF HER PRESENCE WHEN SHE GOT TRAPPED, HE IGNORED ALL THE SCREAMS AND CRUSHED HER TO DEATH. HE WAS NEVER TRIED AND ESCAPED ALL PUNISHMENT. RACHEL'S PARENTS SUED THE AMERICAN CATERPILLAR COMPANY FOR SUPPLYING WEAPONS OF WAR.

Feeling brave and feeling pretty
On my way thru Gaza City
Killing kids and dishing death
As a Dozer Driver for the I.D.F.
Carving carnage all around
Perched on high and looking down
As Arab peasants run to ground
I mow down houses, people too
If they dare oppose the chosen few
When I speed up and plough them under
My heavy blade rips them asunder
But I'm so sad when I hear no screams
Over the roar of the monster machines
But a Dozer Driver of the I.D.F.
Can slaughter kids and dish out death
On his way thru Gaza City
Feeling brave and feeling pretty
For we live in a land of milk and honey
That floats on a sea of American money
But we trespass into a stricken land
With tanks and planes at our command

But my favourite toy is my giant bulldozer
And my greatest joy is to knock kids over
As a hero of the I.D.F.
Killing kids and dishing death
Feeling brave and feeling pretty
On my way thru Gaza City

DEDICATED TO THE BUTCHER WITH THE BULLDOZER

Trilogy to the I.D.F.
(Israeli Defence Force)
Part Three

IN APRIL 2003 AN ISRAELI SNIPER WITH THE I.D.F. SHOT 22 YEAR OLD THOMAS HURNDALL WITH HIS HIGH-POWERED TELESCOPIC RIFLE. TOM WAS IN GAZA AS A PEACE VOLUNTEER AND DIED TRYING TO DRAG THREE YOUNG PALESTINIAN CHILDREN AWAY FROM THE LINE OF FIRE. THEY WERE PINNED DOWN BY THE SAME UNIT, IN THE SAME PLACE, WHERE BRITISH CAMERAMAN, JAMES MILLER, 34 WAS SHOT THROUGH THE NECK, THREE WEEKS LATER. BRITISH COURTS LATER DECLARED THESE INCIDENTS TO BE ILLEGAL KILLINGS, AS WAS THE SHELLING OF A BEACH IN GAZA, IN MARCH, WHEN EIGHT MEMBERS OF A PALESTINIAN FAMILY WERE WIPED OUT AT THE SAME TIME AS DOZENS OF OTHERS WERE INJURED AND MAIMED. THE ORGANISATION, HUMAN RIGHTS WATCH, WHO MONITORED THE INVESTIGATION, DECLARED IT A TOTAL WHITEWASH, AS WAS THE BOMBING OF RED CROSS AMBULANCES, REFUGEE CAMPS AND THE U.N. COMPOUND IN LEBANON, IN 2006.

Feeling brave and feeling pretty
On our way through Gaza City
We're heroes of the I.D.F.
Killing kids and dishing death
With telescopic sights I never ever miss
I greet those Arab kids with my supersonic kiss
It was in the Gaza Strip that I became a killer
And my buddy in the unit later killed a Mr. Miller
I was shooting at some kids and nearly got a hit
When some stupid Englishman did his noble bit
Dragging them away from me, out my line of sight
So I simply shot him down, and much to my delight
He fell upon the ground, with a slightly hollow sound
This callow youth of 22, my rifle had brought down
So for little Tommy Hurndall it didn't take a lot
For a medal-winning marksman, just a single shot
Then English Courts declared these were all war-crimes
But murder here is nothing, just a sign of modern times
As the U.S. always claims, we're always in the right

So they give us planes and bombs, that we drop in the night
On crowded refugee camps, and on the Red Cross too
And on the U.N. forces for there's nothing they will do
Because we ride on the back of a Holy Holocaust
And for war-crimes like ours, no-one counts the cost
So if you take your family, for a day-out at the beach
You still won't be safe, you'll still be in our reach
And our long range guns will blow you all to bits
As heroes of the I.D.F. we have to keep our wits
Feeling brave and feeling pretty
On our way thru Gaza City
We're heroes of the I.D.F.
Killing kids and dishing death

DEDICATED TO SGT. TAYSIR HAYB, HERO OF THE I.D.F.

Tides of Time

As changing tides of time
Wash pebbles from the mind
Let them carve a warning sign
Like some secret valentine
For as the wheels of life run dry
Only memories do not die
As grinding on they slowly spin
The threads of life they weave within
Like silken shadows hanging still
Life's illusions hide at will
But hollow hopes can never be
At peace with truth, and never free
'Til peoples of the Earth are one
Like clouds adrift, beneath the Sun

So Lucky

In bandit country, this looks bad
A milk churn rests on concrete slab
So driving by, we cruise so slow
Fingers on triggers, ready to go
But the blast erupts a yard away
To change our lives that fateful day
My face gets smashed against the truck
But I am told I have great luck
With lungs so pierced with shrapnel hits
And bones that are all smashed to bits
I am so lucky, so they say
To just survive that fateful day
With rib-cage collapsed, and ribs all broke
From shrapnel clots I got a stroke
With a broken neck I got last rites
The doctors rarely saw such sights
Blind and deaf, my ears hung down
But I was lucky, not to drown
In my own blood, so they say
So lucky, on that fateful day

TO MICHEAL KELLY, YORKSHIRE LIGHT INFANTRY, BLOWN UP IN SOUTH ARMAGH 1971

Chapter 6
Poems of Animals

DOMINION OF THE BEAST
A CANINE ELEGY
TRIBUTE Á L'OREAL
I AM A FAROE – ISLANDER
SLAUGHTER OF THE SEALS
WHO KILLED MR BEE?
THE SURREY UNION HUNT
WHERE WILD HORSES GRAZE
AS OF HINGES, AS OF WHEELS
EPITAPH TO A FAITHFUL FRIEND

Dominion of the Beast

I've been around a million years
Of other creatures I've no fears
I fear no Gods, or powers that be
I bear contempt for land and sea
I'm devious and cunning raw
And just ignore all moral law
I crush all creatures in my way
Or just abuse them, day by day
No animal can match my strength
Which lets me roam this land at length
But I scar the earth and drain it dry
And if it bleeds ignore its cry
No creature now can match my speed
But in fact they loathe my breed
I'm vicious and I'm full of spite
I kill for pleasure, that's my right
My name is man, I own this land
And I'll destroy it, if I can

A Canine Elegy

There floats around about my bed
A cold and callous mirror where
I see reflections in my head
Where loves and lives therein are laid
To rest within my morning dreams
Wherein the dimly shadowed air
Blent memories mingle in the seams

In mirrored cracks upon the wall
I sense another presence there
As love again comes close to call
I watch the shadows rise and fall
And see a sudden friend appear
That draws from me a tender tear
A faithful dog, who loved me dear

But as the mirror mists with age
I seem to lose all sense of time
This book of life has turned the page
And thoughts now trapped within the cage
Shine in the mirror, love to save
Within my mind, to leave a sign
Thou still he slumbers, in his grave

Tribute Á L'Oreal

I walk in darkness like the night
As innocence and beauty fight
Behind the banner of the Body Shop
For the animal testing will not stop
As subject to these products sold
In testing times so cruel and cold
'Neath the foreign flag of L'Oreal
Countless creatures they do maul
Blinding, burning, none survives
For L'Oreal takes little lives
To test their products rabbits are used
With no tear ducts, they're really abused
As a shampoo dose is put in the eye
They can't flush it out and are just left to die
This truth the Body Shop should tell
As sold for gold when ethics fell
The Body Shop is now deployed
When helpless creatures are destroyed
For animals and ethics all
Are now consumed by L'Oreal

EVERY YEAR THE FRENCH FIRM, L'OREAL, THE LARGEST COSMETIC INDUSTRY IN THE WORLD, TORTURES AND KILLS MILLIONS OF ANIMALS INCLUDING DOGS AND CATS EVEN TO THIS DAY, BECAUSE AS THEY CLAIM IN THEIR ADVERTS "YOU'RE WORTH IT". L'OREAL DEVIOUSLY DENY, TOGETHER WITH THE OTHER GIANT COSMETIC FIRM OF "OLAY" THAT THEY TEST THEIR PRODUCTS ON ANIMALS BUT IN FACT THEY DO TEST THE INDIVIDUAL INGREDIENTS WHICH IS THE SAME DIFFERENCE; SIMILAR TO NAOMI CAMPBELL SAYING SHE WON'T BUY FUR, BUT STILL WEARING IT DOWN THE CATWALK

I Am a Faroe - Islander

I am a Faroe-Islander
In fact, a family man
But when I see a big fat whale
I'll kill it if I can
I've no respect for man or beast
I don't believe in God
My basic instincts are released
In my culture that is flawed
As I plunge my pick into their brain
To kill thousands year by year
A funny thing, it's not for gain
But just for sport, like drinking beer
For we all live in a land of boredom
Where life is always drab and cold
But come and see our island whoredom
And join us, if you be so bold

DEDICATED TO THE WONDERFUL WOMEN OF THE FAROE-ISLANDS, WHOSE NOBLE SUPPORT SUSTAINS THE ANIMALS THEY LIVE WITH

Slaughter of the Seals

Let's watch her sway and walk away
Now she's got that coat at last
She prayed for it for many a day
And now the years have passed
So watch her turn and pause again
To flaunt the coat she reels
It merely cost the souls of men
Who clubbed to death some seals
So watch her float just like a dove
The coat to swing with merry laugh
It merely cost a mothers love
For her new-born baby calf
So watch her smile a little while
Now she's got that coat at last
Then let us take her by the throat
In her smart expensive sealskin coat
And grind her smile until she spew
In the battered brains and sick remains
Of the carved up martyred few

EVEN TO THE PRESENT DAY CANADA SLAUGHTERS OVER A QUARTER OF A MILLION SEAL PUPS EVERY YEAR BY CLUBBING THEM TO DEATH DESPITE INTERNATIONAL CONDEMNATION.

Who Killed Mister Bee

Did he fly in to say adieu
His visits here were far from new
But trapped beneath my sliding door
Left out of sight, down on the floor
My little dog had heard his cry
So to release him, with a sigh
I nudged the door to edge him free
But Mister Bee just couldn't see
This exit from his agony

He dug in deeper and buzzed back at me
And I heard him so clear, vibrating with fear
But a crisp crunch arose, as I moved the door left
And I knew Mister Bee now of life was bereft
Crushed by my mindless blindness of eye
No longer his fate to fly high in the sky
Spreading pollen and life wherever he went
To what whimsy of fate was his innocence rent

But who killed Mister Bee, was it little dog Bruce
Who caused him to hide, when free and when loose
Beneath sliding doors where I just couldn't see
The cold callous runners that crushed Mister Bee
Was it God who decided his race had been run
Sipping nectar from flowers was just too much fun
Was it me, or my dog, or was it my God
That caused all his strife, or was it simply just life

The Surrey Union Hunt

DEDICATED TO BRIAN WHITE, AND THE OTHER WORKERS OF "STEETLY CHEMICALS", BAYNARDS; RUDGWICK SURREY WHO TRIED TO FIGHT OFF A HORDE OF FOXHOUNDS WITH GARDEN RAKES, AS THEY RIPPED APART A DEER, WHEN IT WAS CORNERED OUTSIDE THEIR WORKPLACE. ONE OF ITS LEGS HAD BEEN TORN OFF AND ITS STOMACH WAS HANGING OUT, AND ALTHOUGH IT WAS ALIVE AND STILL SCREAMING, THE MASTER OF THE "SURREY UNION HUNT", MRS ROSEMARY PETERS, STOOD BY WITH HER ENTOURAGE, AS HER HOUNDS TORE THE DEER TO PIECES.

His velvet antlers pierced the sky
His dappled beauty graced the eye
As he drank from the stream he listened long
To the mournful calls that lit the dawn
But gentle eyes grew wide with fear
As he heard the hounds, so close, so near
Then the horde of horses crested the hill
The hunters brave had found their kill
So he ran for life in full retreat
As stones and rocks tore round his feet
But they ran him to ground at a frantic pace
And swarmed around as he turned to face
A four footed demon straight from hell
With frothy fangs and fearsome yell
That jumped for the throat of this creature fair
And clung in a frenzy threshing the air,
'Til the whining rabble found courage anew
And together, as one, in a pack they threw
Themselves on their victim, to tear and to chew
And as they snarled and ripped and rent
The hunt leered on, its lust well spent

Where Wild Horses Graze

Into the mincer, our new chicks are dumped
For before they hatch out, full of germs they are pumped
And our pigs all scream out, with this terrible sound
When they are held down, by four men on the ground
So a gallon of blood may be drained from each beast
And used to breed germs, like some sort of yeast
Where wild horses graze, you cannot get near
So you can't see their plight and you can't feel their fear
But the size of the lumps, on the neck of a horse
As its life-blood is drained, for science of course
Has made me ashamed to work in this place
For I sold out my soul, for this sick human race

WELCOME RESEARCH LABORATORIES

As of Hinges, as of Wheels

It is of prime concern, when dealing with this firm
That the buildings and the people are all kept well in line
And whitewashed and well polished so that time after time
On all the guided tours where there's always lots of space
You will never see a thing, in or out of place
But you still might hear a sound, as all around it reels
A squeaking, or a creaking, as of hinges, as of wheels
But take a wrong turning, and soon you'll sense the smell
Of death and of decay, creeping down a deep stairwell
Along the cold dark passages, where tier after tier
Of animals are stacked, in metal racks of fear
They swiftly sense your presence as they seize upon your eyes
And halt you in your tracks, when the screaming starts to rise
As you pass by all their cages, stacked up row by row
The screeching and the screaming simply seems to grow
But don't look at their eyes, just try and hold your breath
And quickly pass them by, these slaves awaiting death
But do pause for a while, as the ringing in your ear
And that lump within your throat, all begin to clear
Like the noise that fades away, you can now begin your day
But you will often feel their fear, and even taste their hate
Long after you have left, and they have met their fate
And at night asleep, you might often-times dream deep
Of a strange and sudden sound, as all around it reels
A squeaking, or a creaking, as of hinges, as of wheels

WELCOME RESEARCH LABORATORIES

Epitaph to a Faithful Friend

Thou not quite dead, so still he lies
As round his head swoop steely flies
So aged and old, yet still he breathes
For not quite cold, his chest still heaves
He loved to walk in the woods so deep
And he didn't talk, but loved to sleep
He'd walk for miles and never tire
Then hurry home to sit by fire
His hair had knots, he loved old socks
And a mouldy chair where he'd watch the box
But he grew housebound when he lost his sight
And he'd bump around in his endless night
Then he stiffened up, with joints like lead
So from plastic cup and bowl he fed
But he gave and got a lot of love
And he still loved life, with all its strife
So he stuck it out 'til the final shout
He so loved life, this little man
As only a canny canine can

Chapter 7
Poems of Poverty

POVERTY
THE RUNAWAY
ON HIS OWN
UNEMPLOYED
THE IMMIGRANT
HER USUAL SELF
THE BABY SMILES
DEATH OF A FRIEND
THE PHONE-BOX BOY
THE WORLD PASSED BY

Poverty

Poverty stalks my dreams in the night
As he walks on the beach, 'tween tides of time
He shelters in shadows, away from the light
And thou I can't see him, he follows my line
And nothing I do will make him take flight

But as he circles, sheltered in shade
I wander along to his old Devil song
And hear him and fear him and feel so afraid
For I wonder to whom my soul will belong
As he lurches along the trail I have made

Dragging Demons for me out the sack on his back
While I just need to sleep in dark dunes of sand
But he waits 'til I stagger to start his attack
Then seizes me tight in the grip of his hand
As the seams of my dreams all fade into black

So we wander along, shackled together
To shuffle the shore, at a slovenly pace
With Conscience in tow, whatever the weather
For she's in no hurry to finish the race
With a hold of my soul, her song is forever

But stumbling on stones thrown up by the sea
My nemesis Death is heading this way
He digs up old wounds to hurl them at me
As stalking beneath this sky of slate-grey
He callously casts them with vigour and glee

Now I spot his companions Illness and Fear
Who are lurking close by, waiting to show
Their slow recognition, as we grow near
But now I do fear, they will deal me a blow
So I fight against Fate, to escape and get clear

But they come within reach, so we sit on the beach
In a hollow called Hope, where we celebrate Hate
A faithful old friend, who seems to be late
But the party has started, and will go on 'til dawn
When they all will decide, just to whom I belong

The Runaway

This thing that perched upon the edge
And waited on the pavement ledge
Stared out blankly at a world
Where the callous rush of life unfurled
A youth whose callow innocence lay tousled in the wind
To float amidst the dust, where like a dream it spinned
An echo in the street, a slow and strangled call
That tightened in his throat, as it beat against the wall
A sound that gave me guilt to sense its quiet embrace
As he stalked along the street and I saw his frightened face
When he entered slow this city, devoid of love or pity
And realised existing, or surviving in this place
Would stop his soul reviving, faith in the human race

DEDICATED TO THE THOUSANDS OF TEENAGERS, SLEEEPING ROUGH

On His Own

With the drift of the snow came the night closing fast
And full well he knew, that his fire would not last
So he wrapped in his rags and left the dying heat
Little thinking that night, his death he would meet
He had lived by himself, preferred being alone
And never spoke much, except just to moan
But that's why he died, not of cold, on it's own
But more of the fact that he stayed so alone
They found him that night, by the street lamp above
He had died from the lack of something called love

CARDBOARD CITY WATERLOO 2003

Unemployed

Sleeping late, eating less
Today, tomorrow, just a guess
Unemployed, on the dole
One of millions, playing a role
An interview at the crack of dawn
Hope to God it won't take long
For another job would go down fine
Being out of work is such a crime
So looking smart, but feeling a fool
I turn up on time and try to look cool
Please take a seat, just wait a minute
Don't worry, I say, a minute's not in it
This year, the minutes, the worry, the fear
Of living alone without any money
Isn't so funny, a minutes not in it
Hope to God I'll be working soon
Go in now, it's the first on the right
A roomful of losers, washed in the light
Filling in forms, on what's wrong and what's right
But after a while, in we all file
Tightening our tie and flashing our smile
You must understand, the tribunal say
The Job Centre sent you all here today
For the wages are low and the hours really long
And we only want people with brains and with brawn
For with hundreds of people willing to work
We have to make sure you're not going to shirk
There's a short list, you see, of workers to be
So run along, you lucky man
Run from the system while you still can
Just look for our letter, tomorrow at noon
And we do hope you find what you're looking for soon

The Immigrant

Pity the poor immigrant,
With no uncle, with no aunt
And no family he can see
All alone now he will be
With so few jobs that he can take
Will poverty be hard to shake
Will he ever end up rich
No, only with a lottery glitch
And will a life of pain and drink
Drive him to the very brink
Or will this time so full of grime
Drive him to a life of crime
And will he ever find a wife
Or will his life be full of strife
Will gentle hands smooth out his hair
Or is his fate the barbers' chair
No soothing voice for an aching head
Just a bottle of booze and a lonely bed
No hospital visits whenever he's ill
Just nurses with needles and pill after pill
No loving caress, that to him meant so much
Now just an old memory he never can touch
No welcoming arms or children's glees
Just a tired old dog all covered in fleas
No breakfast in bed with the Sunday news
Just four empty walls to echo his views
No family Mass with the choir in full song
Just a drink in the pub and a sad sing-a-long
No visits from sons or daughters today
Just a friendly drunk to usher away
No cosy fire with logs all alight
Just a one-bar heater to lighten the night
At Christmas, no crackers or brandy pudd
Just a T.V. dinner that looks rather rude
No green Christmas tree lit up with lights

Just the echoes of neighbours having their fights
No walks in the wood or romps in the snow
With no-one around there's no-where to go
So to live in this place and not drown in despair
He will need to pursue a life full of prayer
For left on his own in this awful land
He surely will need some guiding hand

Her Usual Self

TO THE MEMORY OF BEVERLY LEWIS, WHO DIED AT THE AGE OF TWENTY-THREE, ON THE SEVENTEENTH OF FEBRUARY, NINETEEN EIGHTY-NINE. SHE WAS A BLIND AND DEAF SPASTIC WOMAN WHO LIVED IN A BACK ROOM, SLEEPING ON AN OLD SETTEE COVERED WITH NEWSPAPERS; WHEN SOCIAL SERVICES VISITED THE HOUSE MR. KIETH PARRY, OF GLOUCHESTERSHIRE COUNTY COUNCIL, SAID BEVERLY HAD BEEN IN THAT CONDITION FOR SO LONG SHE SHOULD BE USED TO IT, BECAUSE THE HOUSE WAS LITTERED WITH OLD NEWSPAPERS AND ROTTING FOOD. BEVERLY WAS GENERALLY LEFT NAKED BUT WAS OCCASIONALLY CLOTHED IN A BLANKET, OR A BUNDLE OF OLD MATERIALS. WHEN FOUND SHE WEIGHED LESS THAN FOUR STONE.

I never saw her again
But, when I went there last
She was her usual self
And all that was needed
Was merely to move her
From the settee to a mattress
We did try, the Doctor and I
But it was difficult to breathe
With death and decay
Eating up the air
Besides we had to peel away
So gently off her back
A filthy rotting sack
Which served to keep her warm
For she was blind and deaf, of course
Which did help to explain
Why she never felt the pain
Of being welded by her waste
Itself a sticky paste
That sucked her down
With every breath
Into an evil pit of death
Now the sound of her shame
As she gently froze in pain
Will never ever leave
And now I dare not think of her
Except when I see snow or rain
Slide gently down my window pane

The Baby Smiles

In the wind and rain
The baby smiles
The rain
Coats her smile
With tears
I wonder
Will the tent
Hold out the cold
For with hunger
The little ones
Cry such a lot
But the baby is good
She does not cry
For now I see
She cannot feel
The wind or rain
Or the hunger
Or my love
The rain
Coats her smile
With tears

BANGLADESH OCTOBER 1988

Death of a Friend

Strong of hand, fleet of feet
For guys like us, all life was sweet
We'd dance and drink 'til the early hours
Then sleep in the park after picking the flowers
Of women and wine, we had our fill
But time pushed us both, right over the hill
Booze got the better of Bob, there's no doubt
For his family and friends soon wanted out
He wound up in a hostel for addicts and drunks
I went to an Abbey and lived with the monks
Bob slept on his shoes, as a pillow at night
As bugs drained his strength, by the moon's misty light
His bed lay in a row, in a big hollow room
Where at night naked men would all pee in the gloom
Now his comrades in dreams were armies of mice
And they shared this great feast with scabies and lice
To escape from this world Bob then turned to drugs
Which we both had agreed were only for mugs
Yet one night he drowned, in their tender caress
But grateful I was, that he died without stress

IN MEMORY OF MY DEAR FRIEND ROBERT COLEMAN

The Phone Box Boy

They called me that, for I had been found
Wrapped in a blanket, lying on the ground
In a red phone box, in the dead of the night
As the moon and my mum slid out of sight
Barnardoes turned up and gave me a home
But as I grew up I just wanted to roam
Here life was too noisy, I was never alone
So I left there, with nothing to carry but pride
And a strong sense of ethics, deep down inside
With no family or friends I would sleep in a ditch
But on all village greens, my tent I could pitch
For I'd found a friend, as I travelled round
Relating my tales to folks that I found
My friend was a donkey, and he pulled a cart
And for many long years he lived in my heart
We would travel the land, sleeping under the stars
Local by-laws allowed me to build little fires
On all village greens, so we could rest up
To cook us a meal, and sit there and sup
And then tell our stories, as folk filled our cup
With pennies and pity, and wishes of luck
'Til one night we camped by Blewbury Green
And I told my tales 'neath a frozen moon-beam
When three little lads, barely teens, I am told
Cornered old Merlin, as he lay tired and cold
With hands ever gentle, they stroked his long tail
But with evil intent for they made Merlin wail
When they tied on fire-crackers, and giggled in glee
As they then lit them up, when no-one could see
Merlin frothed at the mouth, just gasping for air
And panicked in fear, to run here and run there

But got hit by a truck, that fast homeward bound
Crushed poor old Merlin, right into the ground-
I still haunt the highways, telling my tale
And I will not stop, and I will not fail
To find those three lads, some cold moonlit night
When I'll teach them all, the real meaning of fright

FOR PETER (KULGAN) CAIRNS, AND MERLIN, HIS FAITHFUL FRIEND FOR 17 YEARS, AND OF COURSE, THE GOOD FOLK OF BLEWBURY.

The World Passed By

Stretched out on his bed of papers and wood
The old man lay quietly sighing
He ached at the thought of warmth and food
But the world passed him by and he heard it sigh
Oh dear, what a shame, who's to blame
I'd help if only I could, I would
I'd help for I feel that I should

His legs grew cold as the wind grew bold
For his clothes were all falling apart
He had wanted to go, for it looked like snow
But he hadn't the strength to start
The world passed him by and he heard it sigh
I'd help if only I could, I would
I'd help for I feel that I should

It started to snow as night came on
But the old man was quiet, his hunger had gone
Now he was alone in a world of his own
He'd ended his fast at last
The night passed him by, and it did sigh
I helped for I knew if I could I would
I helped for I felt that I should

THAMES EMBANKMMENT 2004

Chapter 8
Poems of Pain

LETTER TO JOHN
LONELINESS
THE SAGA OF SARITA
ODE TO A MASOCHIST
FAILURE
ANIMAL SLIGHTS
DEPRESSION
DARK FOR ME
COURTROOM NUMBER THREE
THE SILENCE OF THE SLEEPING SCREWS

Letter to John

Dear John
Thank you
For being born
I'm just sorry the world
Cannot offer you more
More peace, more love
More happiness
Just sorry it can't
Promise power
Or hand out
Gifts of glory
Just sorry it won't
Let you be yourself
You will have to hide
Behind a mask to survive
Have to strive hard
To earn money or fame
So that you may keep
Your health and sanity
Sorry this world won't
Bless you without pain
You will have to suffer
Like all the rest
Because this world belongs
To a God who keeps it
Just the way it is
So that all his people
May one day be forced
To turn to him
Usually on bended knees
And furthermore
You're not really my son
You belong to this God
And he does not make life easy
Especially for His sons

TO MY SON JOHN

Loneliness

Loneliness struck me last night in my sleep
I awoke as it struck like a shark from the deep
To sever and seize and slice in surprise
Like a low bridge will catch a bus on the rise
It then filled the void with memories and places
Now those that I loved were simply blank faces
And I was able no longer to look at the sky
So I stared at the floor and just wondered why
I felt guilt in the tick and the tock of a clock
As it swallowed my mind, causing a headache
That grew like the wail of a late paramedic
But watching this world drink long and deep
Made me thirst even more, for some sense of sleep
For I just couldn't see, taste, touch or smell
Now I was alone in my own private hell
Watching water lay dormant, deep down in the well

The Saga of Sarita

We need to tell when you get well
So take these pills and stay in bed
But I don't believe in pills, I said

What will I gain, if I kill all this pain
Pain is an old acquaintance of mine
Who frequently visits to just pass the time

With no announcement, he'll just flounce in
But now I am used to his evil old ways
And simply ignore him, except on damp days

For I knew a few whose friendship he grew
But friendship with him leads only to fear
And when he gets near, you just can't think clear

I once knew a girl, and her life was a whirl
For she gave him gifts, like needles and knives
Which he often would use to take peoples lives

But left on her own, she was never alone
For he gave her badges of loss and despair
That she stuck in her arms until they lay bare

With a clench of her fist, they'd appear on her wrist
Then spread up her arms, 'til they both looked the same
Her friend pain was loyal, more than me, to my shame

When she wasn't well, I would have to break down
With panic and yell, the old bathroom door
To find her poor shell, stuck flat on the floor

I'd slide and I'd slip where her blood would drip
Just wrapping loo-rolls all round her gashes
As her life-blood pumped out, thru scarlet slashes

As I would stumble the roll would fumble
Onto the floor where it's virginal white
Soaked up her life 'neath the pale naked light

She'd wake up next day, feeling ever so gay
But never sought help with a suicide bid
For fear she'd be wired to the National Grid

They took her kids in the end, for they just couldn't fend
But they never got her, for her friend Mister Pain
Paid a visit one night, in the dark and the rain

She felt so alone that she followed him home-
She now slips my mind, 'til I see poppies wilt
Then my vision blurs up, with shame and with guilt

TO SARITA, WHEREVER SHE MAY BE

Ode to a Masochist

In bed she said 'I know it sounds unkind'
You're a slave to your body, not to your mind
A mind so fine, that feeds like fire
Twisting, turning, all desire
With features fair, that blazing pain
Betray you as a blind mans cane

Those eyes like rain, their heady dance
A-prance upon my window pane
Yet still you will your body strong
To screaming silent, screaming long

And so I lost the power of love
As her pregnant silence hung above
The bed, wherein my head was laid
All promise now of the dream gone dead
As we listened long to my oozing breath
Gather in strength for my coming death

Failure

Failure feeds like condensation
With the clinging damp of hesitation
When life itself seeks out revenge
Like loss of trust in faithful friends
And the bravest of men must fade in its gaze
Where wisdom alone can kindle the blaze
Of a God on high that makes men think
As failures, we all in His image shrink
Then faith and hope must surely shake
The thought that God might make mistake
We should then with despair driven
Fall to our knees to be forgiven

Animal Slights

We are special, we are free
We are blest, for you can see
How we treat the beasts that be
We feed cows meat, not only grass
We keep pet fish 'tween sheets of glass
We gas badgers, we eat frogs
We experiment on tortured dogs
We feed our chickens mum and dad
They eat themselves, which can't be bad
We pour acid into rabbit's eyes
But if you ask, we'll tell you lies
We shoot rhinos for horn and bears just for skin
And take elephant tusks that even look thin
We eat monkey brains while they're still alive
It's no miracle none of them ever survive
But when our lengthy race is run
God will remember what we've done
So do not worry, do not fuss
He'll have some special plans for us

Depression

Silence sparkles open my eyes
From the stable of the night
From it's cradle come the cries
Breeding rhapsodies of fright

Now this nakedness I loathe
As the memories of the night
Make her progenies explode
As the light of dawn takes flight

Into vessels of my guilt
That drown my deep resolve
As the reapers of the night
Scythe my reason to dissolve

My senses like the hammer
Of a wild thing in a room
That seeks a craven peace
But must wallow in it's doom

Dark For Me

It was dark when I awoke
To the smell of ether, and
When I opened my eyes
It was still dark, and
When the dawn filtered
Through the curtains
Of my mind
It was still dark, and
When at noon, the sun
Lit my life with fear
It was still dark, and
When it slowly faded
Like my hopes, and
All that I could see
Were dark explosions
Of mystery
It was still dark, and
Now reflecting back
I think somehow
It had always been
In some way
Dark for me

ST. GEORGES EYE HOSPITAL. TOOTING BEC. LONDON

Courtroom Number Three

In Courtroom Number Three I wondered why I sensed
The echoed shout of a lonely seagull scream
As the wind hurled it about, to become part of my dream
In the corridors outside, where hidden in my hand
Lay the bail form, as the band, of freedom fighters fought
An exit from this Court, where I has faced a fine
And aluminium doors, polished with their shine

In Courtroom Number Three I wondered why I sensed
The image and the glitter of the living world outside
So free of debts and litter, where health and wealth decide
As reflections of our pride, from a dim and distant past
So silently were cast, to shimmer 'neath the scene
Of leaden skies above a long lost meadow green
Like a woman's love, within a virgins scream

In Courtroom Number Three I wondered why I sensed
This place where justice flourished and poverty was nourished
Where I saw myself in others, stalking corridors in stealth
My future brothers and their wealth, all locked in some fools hand
With the laws of this fair land, back in Courtroom Number Three
Where we lusted to be free, like that seagull in the sky
And I wondered, and I wondered why

HOVE MAGISTRATES COURT

In the Silence of the Sleeping Screws

Right, Rooney, you're next, pickup at the Prison
For the Hospital Wing, at Wormwood Scrubs
So as the sun comes up, I watch like a vision
As wooden gates hanging, on giant metal lugs
Open and close in this concrete canal
Sifting debris, not ships, and lives cut in bits
And our day-release lag, now cuffed and banal
And suited and fed, is tethered and led
To sit in the back, next to Bill, while fat Phil
Sits up front and free, riding shotgun with me
As he loosens his tie to relax, I can see
Double three-one-two is a really nice guy
Simply strangled his wife and got life, so I sigh
And sit back and think, will he ever be free
And 'but for the grace of God', go we three
So we head up the by-pass, an unrelenting view
From the Hospital Wing for Double three-one-two
But cruising at the Ton, does his heart no good
So I slow right down, but we can't stop for food
But there is some cheese, so we all have a slice
And at the 'Scrubs buy their tie, at the prison price
Then slowly drive on through more metal gates
To the Cardiac Clinic, where we all look like mates
When Phil and Bill shed their coats, to show off tattoos
And chat up the nurses, while the doctors share views
But cruising home in the dark, on a black shiny road
I seize on the chance to lighten my load
Phil and Bill were asleep, as only we knew
And so we shared some secret views
In the silence of the sleeping screws

COURTESY BECKS CAR-HIRE COMPANY LEWES

Chapter 9
Poems of Death

DANCE OF DEATH
DESIGNER DEATH
THE ACCIDENT
THE LIFT
FOR THEM
MY E-TYPE JAG
THE TREE OF LIFE
TYBURN TREE
THE WATCHER
TRILOGY TO A FOETUS

Dance of Death

His wheezing throat sang a mournful note
As his rasping lungs played a tune with his gums
His mechanical chin made a frightful din
As he shut his eyes and shuddered sighs
He muttered the tune like a fluttered balloon
His pulse did race and his sweat-soaked face
Strained his veins like horses reins
This dance of death made him fight for breath
But I saw in his face the end of the race
It grew slack with relief as he ended his grief
His heaving chest was now at rest
And he just passed away, like the light from the day

NORWOOD HOUSE OLD FOLKS HOME, LONDON

Designer Death

Nothing new, in Nature, nor
A bargain at the price

Lacking reason, season, space
Drowning every trace of grace

Cloaking shock in disbelief
Less to accept, this sudden grief

But devious and cunning raw
He extends a tempting claw

To cast afar his loving net
Stretched with pain and sorrow yet

Tensioned by the promised morrow
Some vestige of remorse to borrow

Virgin guilt so sparkling fresh
That calls again to conscious flesh

Those bygone lives that surface fast
Where memories in the pool are cast

As meaning reasons slowly silt
To fill this world so full of guilt

The Accident

I waken slow, what is my fate
I've overslept, I must be late
But now my eyes look round to see
Large pools of blood surrounding me
And now I see lying in the street
Shattered remnants round my feet
And now this blood so fresh and red
Screams out at me, I'll soon be dead

DEDICATED TO TRIUMPH MOTORCYCLES 1975

The Lift

She entered slowly with a sigh
The shuttered concrete building high
The lift she found not far away
To be closed in, on such a day
It sensed just when she was inside
And closed it's jaws to start the ride
But she felt so lonesome there
For humming deep within it's lair
The motor whirred with easy grace
The lift to raise at constant pace
Just four cold walls to touch and see
But she felt she'd soon be free
For when at last she reached the roof
Looking down felt so aloof
Spotting people in the street
Could they see her down beneath?
She walked up to the buildings edge
Her fingers stroked the concrete ledge
She found the ride down slightly quicker
The leering crowd left, slightly sicker

TO JEANETTE 1979

For Them

WRITTEN AT BEACHY HEAD, SUSSEX, THE MOST NOTORIOUS SUICIDE VENUE IN ENGLAND, WHERE ON AVERAGE TWENTY PEOPLE PERISH EVERY YEAR.

For them
The ones,
Who end it all
In last brave acts
The martyred few
Who stand and wait
And hesitate
To shake and shudder
But, do sometimes
Fall, or drown
As the case may be
But why, for what, for us
They do not save themselves
Or any thing or being
But let us kindly hope
In their long last drop
Of no return
As final curtains fall
That they might somehow see
In that fleeting moment
True Peace
Hurtling towards them
From out the tunnel of despair

IN MEMORY OF MY DEAR FRIEND, PETER WIMBLE, 2 FEB 2007 R.I.P.

My E-type Jag

Oh, I do feel a wag
In my E-type Jag
It can do one-fifty
And that is pretty nifty
But if I crash at that speed
Of my remains take no heed
For if I sneeze in the breeze
Or just so much as blink
I shall be dead in a wink
All sprawled on the road
Like a spotted toad
My car will be flat
Like a cricket bat
There'll be nothing left
Of my bowler hat
The people will look
And say, 'fancy that'
But he did feel a wag,
In his E-type Jag

The Tree of Life

Sister saw the tall tree fall
Saw the soul that would not die
Saw the sap of life run dry
And felt the restless breezes fly

She sat and held an arm at length
She slowly mopped a fevered brow
She sensed a slowly fading strength
And felt the weakness in the bough

She held out helping hands to cushion
Branches bending to the Earth
The breeze now sees no leaf to loosen
The soul now seeks another birth

**ON THE DEATH OF MY MOTHER
7th FEBRUARY 1984**

Tyburn Tree

Round Tyburn Tree, impatiently
Awaited the multitude, and me
The star of the show
To appear was slow
But we who had been
There often before
Drank steadily on
Thirsting for more
Then they dragged him forth
To entertain
And hoisted him slow
Screaming with pain
He wriggled and squirmed
And we squealed with delight
When two of his friends
To his legs clung tight
But they quickened the end
For soon he was dead
Later on, one of them
Shot the Judge, so they said
The other paid a visit
To the hangman's wife
And the only thing spared
Was the poor lady's life
His brother, I heard
Cut his wrists apart
When their mother died
From a broken heart
Now his wife walks the streets
Turned into a whore
And the children don't talk
At all, anymore

**COMPOSED UNDER TYBURN TREE,
HYDE PARK CORNER LONDON**

The Watcher

I've been around for eighty years
I've stood and watched in cold and heat
I've seen so many hopes and fears
Cross my path, for roots run deep
So I perch upon this cliff and gaze
At ships far out at sea

While tides flow fast, to my amaze
All sorts of people flock to me
Some shelter from a foreign foe
For I give them warmth and heat
As they scour the beach below
For the enemy they hope to meet

But as seasons came and seasons went
I saw small babes grow into men
Then off to war they would be sent
To be never ever seen again
And near my foot a tattered grave
Of an old friend I had known

When famine came, for food he'd crave
And harvest from the crops he'd sown
But now in truth it must be told
There was a time I hanged a man
He had a choice, this fellow bold
But to my very feet he ran

So they cornered him and hung him high
But I did sigh, as they cut him down
To a whispered cry, from the branch so dry
'Twas a silent sound, as he fell to ground
For my many leaves, now drunk with sorrow
Fell with him, to grace the morrow

Trilogy to a Foetus
A Mothers Love

I wonder what it is they feel
Within the womb that is their seal
Where they float in sacred space
As this warm and precious place
Reverts into an evil tomb
When metal demons probe the womb
To tear apart and rip and rent
As eyes are pierced and skulls are bent
I wonder what it is they feel
As some butcher from above
Their innocence doth steal
I wonder what it is they feel
Could it be a mother's love

Trilogy to a Foetus
The Chosen Few

To them, the chosen few
The dedicated few
The ones that rub and scrub
To operate and slice in pieces
Or even take out whole, the foetus
Not body, mind or flesh
But to them, a bloody mess
Their talent and their skill
Being directed with a will
To mercenary extortions
When they execute abortions

Trilogy to a Foetus
Tonight

Tonight my thoughts I save
Not simply for the brave
Or even the insane
Tonight my thoughts
My pity and my pain
All fall to you
Those conceived few
So full of hope
And loving mirth
Who must return
Unto this Earth
Before they earn
Their rightful birth

DEDICATED TO THE 934,733,000 REGISTERED WORLDWIDE ABORTIONS THIS IS EQUAL TO ONE ABORTION FOR EVERY WOMAN ON THE PLANET. (IN TWO WORLD WARS ONLY 70 MILLION PERISHED)

Chapter 10
Poems of Praise

GOD SO LOVED THE WORLD
I DON'T REMEMBER SINGING
WHEN THE SAINTS GO MARCHING IN
THE AGE OF REASON
I SEE YOU
EVIL IN - EVIL OUT
SHOW ME, LORD
FOR THE LOVE OF GOD
AN ALIEN GOD
BLESS THIS DAY

God So Loved the World

That he gave his sun to sprinkle light
To gently bathe and brighten night
Yet even more soft rains to pour
As sheets of freshness spreading clean
Enlighten life and brighten scene
So when it rains upon ourselves
We should with joy jump off our shelves
Springing down to splash and sing
Where virgin raindrops dance in Spring

I Don't Remember Singing

I don't remember singing
Never knew if I could, or I should
Never had much to sing about
But things could often make me shout
If in my mind, they would annoy
But I never ever felt that joy
That blossomed forth into song
But if I felt I did belong
I'd sometimes hum amidst the throng

But I don't remember singing
Never knew if I could, or I should
In dark streets I'd wander home
And sometimes whistle when alone
But even when I heard a song
I'd puzzle where it did belong
And I would pause along the street
To wonder why they felt so tweet
Was it only me who felt so sad
Or were those singers all quite mad

But once I came across a church
As on a hill I saw it perch
And thru the speckled stainéd glass
Voices strong rose deep in mass
They made me venture to the sound
And once inside, indeed I found
A peace and blessing in their song
And found in time I could belong
Conjoined with them in fervent praise
As now in song my voice I raise
My spirit soars, to my amaze

When the Saints Go Marching In

In life we all have a right to be wrong
But rarely possess a right to belong
Or reap forgiveness for our will
Or force repentance for some ill
But souls in brokenness repent
When sorrow swallows sins consent
Then cleansed and clean we do not drown
But live again, to wear the crown
Redeemed, forgiven, free of guilt
With no conscience left to wilt
While miracles may fade with faith
Truth will survive in God's own Wraith
But while drunks and addicts crave
Will all the saints survive the grave?

The Age of Reason

I felt it one of Gods days
I felt His touch in many ways
I watched the sun rise high to heat
As nature woke from slumber deep

As shadows stalked between the trees
To echo with the gentle breeze
To me a rustling peace they weaved
Yet thinking back my heart was grieved

I sensed that day my youth had passed
For as the dusk came drifting fast
Dark distant bells sang out relief
To sing the sadness of my grief

I See You

I hear you move amongst the trees
As you rustle with the leaves
I see you in the wind and rain
I even feel you in my pain
I hear your whisper in the grave
I watch you on an ocean wave
I smell you thru a fragrant flower
I touch you in a summer shower
I watch you where the swallow flies
As you put colour in the skies
I feel your shadows drift the night
Your grace bestows the stars their light
So surely you will fill my days
With all the wonder of your ways

Evil In – Evil Out

As evil out the shadowed sun
Is drawn from Heavens good to come
Like despair that drugs and dulls
Into indifference love it lulls
For the man who evil feels
Though he revolve within the wheels
Of justice grinding out a shout
To God the evil still will out
And yet the man, the Devil's claimed
Though with stigma may be maimed
If good he feels within his ways
A God on high will bless his days

Show Me, Lord

I am blinded Lord, I cannot see
Let me see peace that I may see love
Let me see pity, where I see only pain
Grant me the freedom, Lord, to listen
In silence, and seek in the shadows, for light
Then show me Lord, your greatness
That I might build a wall of wisdom
Where I might find You, my God
In all forms, of all things, in all men
Then teach me Lord to forgive
All forms of all things in all men
So show me Lord, the good
Show me, Lord, the miracle

For the Love of God

The usual crowd in the usual place
A cold Sunday morning, and no parking space
Nothing seemed special about church today
'Til I forced myself to pray
I paid due homage and then said amen
But knew something different was happening when
God's spirit touched me in some special way
And I felt true peace, like a small child at play
Powerful feelings like this I never had
And feeling such joy I was no longer sad
I had always loved God in my simple way
But now felt ecstatic on that special day
Thou I always could feel His love for me
It was now with a shock I really could see
This feeling I felt for the great God above
Meant clearly to me I was simply in love

An Alien God

Is there an Easter or Christmas on Mars
Or on some distant planet out in the stars
Where a tall bearded wonder preached to a crowd
'Neath the gassy mass of a chlorine cloud
Did twelve faithful followers write what he said
As masses of monsters with manna were fed
When the lame and the halt lost a trunk or a feeler
Did he graft them back on as a miracle healer
Was he then stapled down with relish and glee
By a squawking crowd to a luminous tree
Did he heal beaks and claws just to suffer their scorn
Or did some of them sense that a God had been born

Bless This Day

Bless this day Lord, to my body and my mind
Thank you for what I have, and for what I have not
Lord, grant me a day free of injury and insult
But bless me with the courage of my convictions
And teach me Lord, to control my body and my mind
Give me the strength to forgive others
And the wisdom, oh God, to forgive myself
Keep me safe and sane within your will
But give me the grace, to suffer in silence
That I might live this day, in dignity and peace
Bless the day Lord, until the dark of night
Bless the day Lord, that I might see the light

CLASSICAL HAIKU

*Ten Sets
of Huddles*

Haiku

A HAIKU is an ancient Japanese type of classic three-line proverb, or poem, constrained to seventeen syllables. Five in the first and last lines, with seven in the middle one.

They can be formatted in the English idiom but the number of syllables makes them very limited, and difficult to compose. It is an added bonus if the writer can incorporate a rhyme or two into the Haiku. It is interesting to note that most modern Haiku do not adhere to the classical tradition of 5-7-5.

A 'set' consists of ten Haiku, and traditionally sets are collated in three, six or ten to comprise 30, 60 or 100 Haiku.

The collection that follows comprises ten sets of ten Haiku each. They are sometimes known as "Huddles of HAIKU." The following "Radical Haiku" total ten Huddles of Ten comprising 100 haiku and together with the one hundred poems comprise "The Century Collection".

Chapter 11

Huddle 1

While the acorn drops
The eagle sees, the deer hears
But the insect eats

Time and tide are slaves
To no man, but all men are
Slaves to each other

The most selfish men
Argue most logically
About climate change

What a great teacher
Time is, except that he kills
All of his pupils

No one can fathom
The full and true design of
Their own destiny

Animals possess
That virtue of innocence
Which we humans lack

If it's worth doing
Do it badly, if you can't
Seem to do it well

At any time one may
Practice forms of poetry
The noblest of arts

Life should be counted
In years, not seconds, minutes
Moments, hours, or tears

God let's anything
Happen to just anyone
Anytime or place

Chapter 12

Huddle 2

May your spirit thrive
To survive life's storms, so your
Eyes may shine with peace

It is written that
All men will die in time, but
Few will really live

Envy is cancer
Of the soul, eating spirit
Leaving bitterness

When lost in shadows
Seek the surrounding light that
Casts them over you

Envy the young their youth
But naught else for that is all
They really possess

God created us
For the invention of his
Pleasure and his love

Our noblest virtue
Loyalty, should reign supreme
Except for honour

Every persons life
Betrays a silent vacuum
Only God can fill

The only freedom
On this earth is achieved by
Freedom of the mind

If this world remains
The same, then all its creatures
Will surely perish

Chapter 13

Huddle 3

Single lives flicker
In the stadium of time
Like swarms of flashbulbs

Without Faith you can't
Please God, even with that great
Virtue, Charity

Carelessness combines
With callous indifference
To create cruelty

Everyone was made
To express a side of God
That no-one else can

The stairway to sin
Is steep and dangerous, yet
Easy to travel

Hate will grow from fear
On the poison tree of life
And its fruit is death

We often weep for
Pity, pain and even shame
But seldom for joy

Experience gives
Knowledge and Wisdom in Life
But books may deceive

If you won't believe
In God, it does not mean He
Won't believe in you

Forget birds and bees
Flies and fleas all prove to me
That God must exist

Chapter 14

Huddle 4

A man's tongue is the
Measure of his mind, that rules
In his heart and soul

Beauty is skin deep
But beauty is how we sense
The world we live in

If you seek the Light
You may need to delve deeply
Into the darkness

Wherever you are
Death will never forsake you
He's your closest friend

Never imagine
God cares for your happiness
His aims are nobler

I am astounded
How easy life is for some
And hard for others

Blood is not thicker
Than water but simply much
Harder to wash off

All life slowly sinks
Like a beautiful sunset
Into quiet darkness

Riches do not lie
In wealth, but rather rest in
The bosom of health

We must all suffer
For without pain there can't be
Any compassion

Chapter 15

Huddle 5

It's not the present
That drives men mad, but rather
Fear of the future

Pride is what we like
To see mostly in ourselves
And least in others

Madness in others
Is not as frightening as
Madness in myself

Just think with your heart
To reach the right decisions
And not with your head

The poor hate the past
Lose all hope for the future
And loathe the present

We are but martyrs
To those who follow and who
Will never know us

While most people dream
Of great achievments, some
Awake and do them

God always decides
Who enters your life but you
Decide who leaves it

Life is simply not
Just full of difficulties
But great challenges

You can't choose those things
Which fate decrees you believe
They, in fact, choose you

Chapter 16

Huddle 6

Realities born
Within the dreams of life join
Desire to vision

I want to hate God
For giving man Dominion
Over animals

Human emotions
Stem from either sacrifice
Or pure selfishness

Life passes people
Quickly by, as they slowly
Make great plans for it

Sense it in others
Loneliness is palpable
See it in yourself

You may hide a while
With a smile, but you can't hide
When crippled inside

It's nobler to feel
Too much emotion in life
Than feel too little

We are all destined,
For each and everyone was
A plan in God's mind

Try and aim to live
With dignity, rather than
Simply die with it

If you are happy
In this world, you're either sick
Silly or just blind

Chapter 17

Huddle 7

Like the planets gaze
On the stars, I was born to
Worship from afar

Prayer does not change
Anything; it changes God
And he changes things

I learnt long ago
That my loyal friend fate was
Just really my foe

God alone decides
When some man or creature dies
Where their spirit lies

Life is mapped not by
Latitude or longitude
But by suffering

One life and one death
Life is death's preparation
Death is simply Gods'

Faith is just the root
The stem that prospers is hope
The flower is love

Waves rise up and fall
Into the sea, to die; man
Does the same, on Earth

We always ask God
For too much, always settling
For far too little

To recognise Good
You may need to encounter
Forces of Evil

Chapter 18

Huddle 8

Ingratitude is
The enemy of Virtue
And the friend of Pride

An eye for an eye
Means simply and finally
Everyone goes blind

It's not suffering
That makes one doubt one's faith, but
Senseless suffering

Though you move mountains
With little love in your heart
You and God must part

Sanity is just
A matter of degree but
Wisdom offers truth

Mans faith grants not grace
But his strength of search, on earth
In this human race

Forgiving others
May be hard, but forgiving,
Yourself, much harder

Character when fed
By suffering is led, to
Hope, when faith is bred

Even a stopped clock
Is right twice a day, so don't,
Dismiss anyone

We are probably
Not the first prototypes, but
We may be the last

Chapter 19

Huddle 9

The shortest distance
Between two points is simply
A nervous breakdown

Hurt can cause Anger
Which can generate Courage
Which can inspire Hope

Love that sings is Praise
Love that leaves is Affection
Love that gives is Grace

Faith and fear will steer
In different directions
The fate of us all

Each passing moment
Is another chance to change
One's life completely

Everything that lives
On this earth was created
Just for God's pleasure

The most beautiful
Things must be felt by the heart
Neither seen nor heard

To further ideas
We must face opposition
Or else we stagnate

To animals relate
Or God will seal your fate, for
All he did create

If you cannot lose
Your past, you may never find
Your proper future

Chapter 20

Huddle 10

The essence of life
Is God, whose essence is Love
To live, you must love

Pride is an excess
Of power, but true Evil
Is excess of Pride

The way we destroy
Our own species, separates
Us from animals

Fear God and not men
To find the wisdom in Life
Wherever you can

Did powers benign
Make birds sing so fine, or did
God, who gave them wings

Animals return
Much more love than they receive
Humans, so much less

Wisdom can just be
Not knowing all the answers
Each and every time

We are sparks, that float
In darkness, glowing briefly
With glimmers of light

What good is wisdom
If you cannot apply it
To any knowledge

Poems lasts forever
Great buildings and monuments
All perish with time

About the Author

J.A.D Rooney

Radical Rooney, as he prefers to be known, especially to the Taxman, was born and bred on the Falls Road, in Belfast, where he grew up in the fifties. To find work he had to immigrate to England, as a teenager, where he took up residence under Clacton Pier for the next six months. After varied jobs in England he then went to work on a Kibbutz and later travelled to the States where he worked for a while before returning to England. He currently lives on his own but was twice married, most recently in a Hot Air Balloon, and has applied for entry in "The Guinness Book of Records", as he believes he was the first person to do this; the wedding actually took place on the very same day that Princess Diana was tragically killed. He also hopes to gain a listing in the book for being the first published poet to hold a public poetry reading on the continent of Antarctica.

He developed an interest in Photography and Writing and became a Technical Author, and published his own glossy magazine `Your Eyes' in Brighton. His articles have been widely published and his poems have appeared in various anthologies, like South East Arts. He wrote a Photography column for `Sussex Scene' and Hastings Council wish to use some of his 'photos in their new brochure about Alexandra Park. His new book 'Travels in Kenya and Egypt' includes hundreds of photographs and will be published later this year. (2008.)

He was sponsored by Hampstead Council for a photography exhibition and some of the work sold there now hangs in Japan and America. He has read at `The Poetry Society' in Earls Court, and at numerous other venues, mainly Pubs and Clubs, and Poetry venues. He has been interviewed on radio and read for Southern Sound on a number of occasions. He is currently compiling an autobiography, and a novel "For the Love of Dog", and a collection of short stories entitled "Tall Tales and Short Stories".

He has acquired many other interests and hobbies, among them Rifle shooting at Bisley and he has a full class `A' Amateur Radio Licence, (G4-PXZ) having spoken to people around the world before mobile 'phones even had a glint in their LEDs. He was recently written up by the Observer, as he happened to communicate with the Space Shuttle Columbia, receiving a QSL card from them before their tragic demise.

He has a number of Patents to his credit, and holds a current Press Card, having been a member of the N.U.J. for longer than he cares to remember. He feels he is sustained by his Faith and love of God. He spends much of his time helping the homeless in soup kitchens.

He has set up his own Domain, 'radicalrooney.com' , and operates through a high speed Hosting in London, as he offers a high quality free photograph, from his archive, with every voiceover of any of his poems. He has no formal qualifications, but joined 'Mensa' in 2005, having had his IQ. rated at one-five-five. He was so surprised by this result that he decided to stop wasting time and compile a book of poetry from the many thousands of poems he has written and this book is the result of those efforts. Combining as they do, ten sets of poems on ten different subjects, together with one hundred classical Haiku these comprise "The Century Collection". His new novel, 'For the Love of Dog' will be released by Authorhouse in 2009.

Index of Poems

Aberfan	32
Animal Slights	102
An Alien God	130
Armageddon	60
As of Hinges, as of Wheels	78
As One	16
Auschwitz	53
Autumn Leaves	38
A Canine Elegy	71
Bless This Day	131
Courtroom Number Three	105
Dance of Death	108
Dark For Me	104
Death of a Friend	91
Depression	103
Designer Death	109
Dominion of the Beast	70
Epitaph to a Faithful Friend	79
Evil In – Evil Out	127
Failure	101
Firestorm Over Dresden	59
First Born	22
Forgotten Love	21
For Them	112
For the Love of Dog	15
For the Love of God	129
God So Loved the World	122
Her Usual Self	89
Hiroshima	50
Huddle 1	135
Huddle 2	137
Huddle 3	139
Huddle 4	141
Huddle 5	143
Huddle 6	145
Huddle 7	147
Huddle 8	149

Huddle 9	151
Huddle 10	153
Infatuation	20
In Dreams	18
In the Cocktail Bar	31
In the Silence of the Sleeping Screws	106
I Am a Faroe - Islander	73
I Am Change, I Am Life	41
I Don't Remember Singing	123
I Fail to Understand	45
I See You	126
Letter to John	96
Let Me Paint	23
Loneliness	97
Loves Return	14
Monkey Business	11
My E-type Jag	113
Nine Eleven	36
Ode to a Masochist	100
On His Own	85
Poverty	82
Progeny	17
Rainbows End	43
Relics of the Past	2
Revelation	47
Sad and Insane	56
Ships in the Night	30
Show Me, Lord	128
Slaughter of the Seals	74
So Lucky	68
The Accident	110
The Age of Reason	125
The Baby Smiles	90
The Culling of a Child	29
The Disappeared	34
The Final Harvest	39
The Hell of Heysel	33
The Immigrant	87
The Irony of Life	9

The Key of the Door .40
The Kings Cross Tube 26
The Leaves in My Fire 44
The Lift 111
The Metaphysical Traveller 8
The Norm 6
The Phone Box Boy .92
The Playground 46
The Rasta-ferry Man .10
The Rose 48
The Runaway 84
The Saga of Sarita 98
The Surrey Union Hunt 76
The Train 4
The Tree of Life 114
The Truth of the Truce 54
The Unsung Stranger 35
The Watcher 116
The Wedding at Port Harcourt 57
The World Passed By 94
The Wrinkled Young 7
Thru Factory Gates 3
Tides of Time 67
Titanic 28
To Him Who Waits .19
Tribute Á L'Oreal 72
Trilogy to a Foetus A Mothers Love 117
Trilogy to a Foetus The Chosen Few 118
Trilogy to a Foetus Tonight 119
Trilogy to the I.D.F. (Israeli Defence Force)Part One .61
Trilogy to the I.D.F. (Israeli Defence Force)Part Two 63
Trilogy to the I.D.F. (Israeli Defence Force)Part Three 65
Tyburn Tree 115
Unemployed 86
When the Saints Go Marching In 124
Where Wild Horses Graze 77
Who Killed Mister Bee 75
With Water in My Eyes 5